CALLED TO THE MINISTRY

by
Edmund P. Clowney

PRESBYTERIAN AND REFORMED PUBLISHING CO.
PHILLIPSBURG, NEW JERSEY

Called to the Ministry
by Edmund P. Clowney

Copyright, 1964, by
Edmund P. Clowney

ISBN: 0-87552-144-4

PRINTED IN THE UNITED STATES OF AMERICA

Contents

Introduction

What is Christ's calling to you? You may be seeking an answer; you may be avoiding the question, but when the Lord calls he will be answered. God's call came suddenly to Elisha; he was plowing a field when Elijah cast the prophet's mantle on him. Levi was in a toll booth, and Peter held a fishing net when Jesus called them.

But how does the Lord call today? You have not been blinded by a heavenly light on the road to Damascus, but you are ready to say with Saul of Tarsus, "Lord, what wouldst thou have me to do?" How does the Lord answer that question?

To begin with, it is clear that the answer must come from the Lord himself. Self-esteem and popular acclaim are treacherous indicators. Christ's spoken word no longer sounds by the lake of Galilee, but he has not left his disciples without direction. We have his written Word in the Bible. Through prophets and apostles Christ's Spirit has testified of him. Where the road forks, the Word of God is the lamp for our feet.

What does the Bible say about Christ's calling? We are told that the Lord calls us by name; every Christian has his or her own calling, a calling as a child of God and a servant of God. Our calling by name gives us our identity and our task.

We must first consider the Lord's calling of every Christian, then we should examine what the New Testament says about the calling of the minister of the gospel.

Part One

WHAT IS GOD'S CALLING?

1.

CALLED BY NAME:
Calling Is God's Creative Gift

To understand your calling, consider what you are called. What is your name, your real name? That name may not appear on your driver's license. Centuries have passed since English names described men's vocations. George Baker became a plumber without becoming a Plumber, and we have no Charlie Astronauts or even Jack Druggists. A son bears his father's name whether it is Robertson, Johnson, or simply Smith. He also has a "given" name that his father (or mother) chose for him.

What's in a name? The answer depends on whose name you bear, and who does the naming. A son may be proud of his father's name; a new bride may find unusual meaning in "Mrs. Robert Jones." Yet our names have become conventional, having no meaning in themselves. Literary fancy may name a boy "Cassius," or prudence may prefer "Mortimer," in the hope that Uncle Mort may revise his will. But usually our names mean nothing at all.

Not so when God names a man. When God calls by name, that name is his calling. Your real name is the name God has given you. Understand that name, and your vocation is set before you. You have two Christian names, and both of those names are "given." Of these God-given names, the last always comes first, and every Christian bears it. That name marks you as a son of God, for it is God's own name. "Bring my sons from far, and my daughters from the end of the earth; every one that is called by my name, and whom I have created for my glory, whom I have formed, yea, whom I have made" (Isa. 43:6b, 7).

A. CALLED BY GOD'S NAME

Every Christian has had God's name solemnly given to him. He has been baptized into the name of the Father, the Son, and the Holy Ghost. Whenever he goes to church, the triune name of God is pronounced upon him again in the blessing of the benediction. In commanding the blessing of his name to be used by the Old Testament priests, God said: "So shall they put my name upon the children of Israel; and I will bless them" (Num. 6:27).

This is the first question of your calling. Do you bear God's name? In the Old Testament temple, the priest wore a golden plate in his turban, carrying the inscription, "Holiness Unto the Lord." In the heavenly Mount Zion of John's vision, the saints of Christ have his name and his Father's name written on their foreheads (Rev. 14:1). John sees one grim alternative: the mark of the Satanic beast on the foreheads of small and great, rich and poor, free and bond (Rev. 13:16).

It must come to that. Neutral anonymity is not possible for man, made in God's image. He must worship or blaspheme.

Salvation means that God writes his name on your head, your hand, your heart. He makes his name yours by making you his. His calling comes with power. Ezekiel saw the mass grave of the people of God. Dry bones filled death valley all about him. But the prophet was moved to cry, "O ye dry bones, hear the word of the Lord!" — and there was resurrection before his eyes (Ezek. 37). God is not God of the dead but of the living; his name is life.

Christ's call reached Zaccheus curiously perched in a sycamore tree: "Zaccheus, come down." It reached Lazarus hopelessly sealed in a tomb: "Lazarus, come forth."

Has that call reached you? There is no call to the ministry that is not first a call to Christ. You dare not lift your hands to place God's name in blessing on his people until you have first clasped them in penitent petition for his saving grace. Until you have done that the issue you face is not really your call to the ministry. It is your call to Christ.

Don't seek the ministry to save your soul. The Lord commits the gospel to the keeping of those who have committed themselves to his keeping (II Tim. 1:12, 14). A man cannot earn his salvation by preaching that salvation cannot be earned. Claim Christ's promise: "He that cometh unto me I will in no wise cast out." He will receive you, and make his name yours forever.

"Who hath saved us, and called us with an holy calling, not according to our works, but according to his own purpose and grace, which was given us in Christ Jesus before the world began" (II Tim. 1:9).

Not a lifetime, not even an eternal-lifetime, can measure the span of God's calling. Like a rainbow, it arches from horizon to horizon. God's life-giving call of grace is the source of our salvation; God's life-shaping call to glory is the goal of our salvation. Indeed, the bow of our own calling reflects the uncreated light of God's grace shining from the dawn before all mornings. With awe the Christian confesses: "Behold what manner of love the Father hath bestowed upon us that we should be called the children of God, and such we are" (I John 3:1).

God's children are called to be like God. Whoever bears God's holy name must be a "holy one," a saint. It is not enough for him to pray, "hallowed be thy name." He must hallow God's name in a life that fulfills his calling. "Like as he who called you is holy, be ye yourselves also holy" (I Pet. 1:15).

The call of the Old Testament saints to walk with God was often set in their names. They carried the divine name "El" or "Jah" in witness to their calling. "Elijah" means "My God is Jah." "Joshua" and "Isaiah" declare that the Lord saves. Israel, Samuel, Hezekiah, Josiah, Nehemiah, and Zechariah all were joined to God by name. If they disobeyed the Lord their God, they dishonored his name. If, like Elijah, they were filled with zeal for the Lord, their lives preached the texts of their names.

God's grace goes even further. Not only does he give his name to his people, but he takes their names as his own. He reveals himself as "El-Elohe-Israel," God, the God of Israel. He is the God of Abraham, Isaac, and Jacob. By the names of his sons, God is identified to the nations.

Did God's goodness exceed his wisdom? Could he not forsee the consequences of identifying himself with this people? God's people defiled his name and made it a vain oath among their conquerors. God's name was blasphemed among the nations precisely because he was known as the God of Israel.

No, God's grace was not in vain, nor was his purpose thwarted. He calls to the distant nations and the isles of the sea to hear his proclamation. He has called from the womb a true Servant who is his salvation to the ends of the earth. This Servant is named of God (Isa. 49:1). He will be the true Israel; he will restore a remnant of the tribes of Jacob and be a light to the Gentiles (Isa. 49:6). His name is Wonderful, Counselor, the Mighty God, the Everlasting Father, the Prince of Peace (Isa. 9:6). He is Immanuel, God with us (Isa. 7:14).

God's purpose to put his name on man in the calling of sonship is realized in Christ. His name is Jesus (Joshua) for he shall save his people from their sins. God's name is in him, and his calling to sonship glorifies his Father's name (Matt. 17:5; John 12:28).

At last God's name is vindicated as El-Elohe-Israel. God's name is revealed in his Son. We know God as the Father of our Lord Jesus Christ (Rom. 15:6).

Blasphemy took the name of Jesus, nailed it above him on the cross, and mocked the Son of God. But God's suffering Servant vanquished even the blasphemy of Calvary: "He saved others, himself he cannot save" (Matt. 27:42). By his death Jesus Christ wrenched that jeer from his mockers and made it gospel truth. Because he would put the holy name of his Father upon sinners, he must bear their sins in his own body on the tree.

Your calling to sonship, to bear God's name, to be a holy one, is your calling in Christ. The time foretold by the prophet has come to pass. A man again may say, "I am Jehovah's." He may write on his hand, "Unto Jehovah" and surname himself with the name of Israel (Isa. 44:5). The wall dividing Jew and Gentile is broken down, for there is but One who is the true son of Abraham. Only in him can anyone be an Israelite indeed, and in him *anyone* can be an Israelite indeed.

The calling of God to bear his name has become the calling of Christ to bear *his* name. His disciples, filled

7

with the Spirit after his resurrection, rejoiced when they were counted worthy to suffer shame for that name.

Your calling is the high calling of God in Christ Jesus (Phil. 3:14). You are accepted in God's beloved Son (Eph. 1:6); you are made holy in Christ Jesus, called to be a saint with all that call upon the name of our Lord Jesus Christ in every place (I Cor. 1:2).

B. CALLED BY YOUR NAME

Your last name, then, comes first. Your name is *Christian,* and in Christ you are called by God's name. You have been brought from far, as the prophet promised, for you have been created for God's glory, and he has brought you to himself.

What then of your first name? That, too, is given to you by God. The Lord who calls you by *his* own name also calls you by *your* own name: "Fear not, for I have redeemed thee; I have called thee by thy name, thou art mine" (Isa. 43:1).

This name, too, is given us in Christ. "Thou shalt be called by a new name, which the mouth of the Lord shall name" (Isa. 62:2). When Jesus called Simon, the fisherman, he gave him a new name: Peter, the "rock." That name did not describe him as he was; it called him to what he would become as the disciple of Christ.

The newness of Christ's salvation is shared by the people of God. The new Israel is called *Hephzibah,* "my delight is in her" (Isa. 62:4).

Have you ever lost interest in Bible reading when you came to the endless names of the Book of Numbers, or the genealogies of Genesis or Chronicles? You may stumble in pronouncing those strange names, but you would not want a Bible without them. God's people are known by name. Their names are recorded in the book of his covenant, and he remembers. The very writing of

8

the names is a memorial of the faithfulness of God. As the names of the tribes of Israel were written upon the precious stones in the breastplate of the high priest when he stood before the Lord to pray, so the names of the true people of God in all their generations are written in God's book (Ex. 28:9-12, 17-21; 32:32; Ps. 56:8; 69: 28).

Psalm 87 celebrates the great day of salvation when God sums up his census books of the citizens of Zion. Then it will be found that Egyptians, Babylonians, Philistines, Tyrians, and Ethiopians have birth records in the city of God. The former enemies of Israel are among those who will sing, "All my fountains are in thee!"

Paul echoes this exultation as he writes to Gentiles in the Roman colony of Philippi: Euodia, Syntyche, Clement, and the rest of his fellow-workers, "whose names are in the book of life" (Phil. 4:3). Not one is forgotten in the book of remembrance written before God for them that fear the Lord and think upon his name (Mal. 3:16).

It is well to reflect on the fact that your individual calling is in the midst of the people of God. You are called individually, but not alone.

But it is *your* name that God calls, and even if it is one of many written in the Lamb's book of life, there in a sense in which it is a secret between you and God. Solomon's God-given name was *Jedidiah,* "beloved of the Lord" (II Sam. 12:25), and the name God gives to you brings not only his blessing but the communion of his personal love. In the Book of Revelation, Jesus promises that to him who overcomes "I will give . . . a white stone, and upon the stone a new name written, which no man knoweth but he that receiveth it" (Rev. 2:17).

The deepest secret of your identity is in that name. Only God knows your real name, but that is the name by which he calls you. The horror of lost identity — namelessness — haunts modern literature. Madison Avenue knows about it, too. A bank recently invited customers from the subway crowds with billboards asserting that at Marine Midland they call account number 9957446, "Harry." How appealing: a city bank with huge resources, but a place where they know me!

Still, there is pathos in that appeal. A man may flee the computers of metropolis to Centerville where everyone will call him, "Harry"—at least everyone who stays on speaking terms with him. Will he then find himself? No, the metropolitan millions serve only to confuse the issue. The tragedy of alienation is not that so many people do not know me; it is that *no one* knows me, for I do not know myself. The terror in modern thought does not spring from the addition of millions in mass population. It springs from the subtraction of One — the Lord my God.

True identity can never come from relations with men, for every relation is a role to be played. To multiply the roles is to fracture the facets of emptiness. To concentrate the roles seems more promising. The man with a few friends and one wife knows more personal involvement than the social butterfly. Yet such involvement cannot engage his whole person, and the man who seeks his identity in love to those nearest him falls into idolatry.

There is but one relation that can give identity to man, the relation to his Creator and Saviour. God's call gives a task that is more than a role, for it engages a man's whole person in the service of his Lord. That call is to being as well as doing, to status as well as service.

Who are you? What are you to do? Both questions are answered in another: By what name does God call you?

Clearly that question will take a lifetime to answer. Peter was given his name, but how little did he grasp its meaning! Only as Christ stretched out his hand to him in the sea, as Christ prayed for him that his faith might not fail, as Christ looked at him in the courtyard of the high priest after Peter's denial, as Christ sat with him by the fire of coals on the beach in Galilee after the resurrection; only in the upper room at Pentecost, in the temple, in the court of the Sanhedrin, in the house of Cornelius; only in the unfolding of his apostolic calling did Peter come to know his name.

You learn to know yourself only as you learn to know Christ. Self-knowledge cannot be an end in itself. Paul never cries with Socrates, "Know thyself!" Rather he says, "That I may know him, and the power of his resurrection, and the fellowship of his sufferings, becoming conformed unto his death; if by any means I may attain unto the resurrection from the dead" (Phil. 3:10, 11). "For to me to live is Christ" (Phil. 1:21) is the text of Paul's life.

2.

CALLED TO SERVICE:

Calling Is God's Royal Bidding

Bearing God's name calls us to serve him. The Christian is a disciple who follows his Lord; Christ's name is his, Christ's way is his, too. The love of sonship delights in service.

A. CALLING TO THE CROSS

"For hereunto were ye called: because Christ also suffered for you, leaving you an example, that ye should follow his steps . . ." (I Pet. 2: 21).

You can never secure in advance a marked tour-guide of your life, but you are shown where Christ's steps lead. They do not go in the way of the world, to fulfill "the desire of the Gentiles" of which Peter speaks in the same epistle. Christ refused that path as often as Satan offered it. Dorothy Sayers, in her play, "The Man Born To Be King," imagines a zealous patriot named Captain Baruch demanding, on the eve of the triumphal entry, that Christ choose between an ass and a stabled war-horse. Let Jesus choose the horse, and Baruch promises a thousand spears behind him as he enters the city; let him choose the ass's colt, and he will ride alone; Baruch will wait for a bolder Messiah.

The steps of Christ go in the path of his Father's calling to suffering and the cross. "For the Son of man also came not to be ministered unto, but to minister, and to give his life a ransom for many" (Mark 10:45). He calls his disciples to the same path: "If any man would come after me, let him deny himself, and take up his cross, and follow me. For whosoever would save his life shall lose it; and whosoever shall lose his life for my sake and the gospel's shall save it" (Mark 8:34, 35).

What vocational guidance can be found in a call to death? Surely death cannot be a calling, but rather ends all calling.

Here the man who follows Christ's steps turns from every other road. Christ's calling was to death. This was the cup given him by the Father. He was the Man of Sorrows, acquainted with grief. Yet he did not suffer to glorify suffering, nor die to sanctify the *mortido,* the death-urge. Nor does he call his disciple to be an idiot of suffering, aimlessly and shamelessly inviting the abuse of every aggressor.

Christ suffered with a purpose. Peter, in the same passage, reminds us that our Lord himself "bare our sins in his body upon the tree, that we, having died unto sins, might live unto righteousness; by whose stripes ye were healed" (I Pet. 2:24).

Christ's suffering was redemptive not because suffering itself is redemptive, but because Christ himself is the Redeemer. The suffering that he endured was for others. He did not need the purging of affliction. He was scourged in the place of sinners that he might heal them; he died in the place of sinners that he might give them life.

The purpose of his suffering was fully accomplished. When Isaiah described the Suffering Servant of the Lord, he did not give a sentimental picture of anguish but told of the triumph of the Sin-Bearer. "When thou shalt make his soul an offering for sin, he shall see his seed, he shall prolong his days, and the pleasure of the Lord shall prosper in his hand" (Isa. 53:10).

For the joy that was set before him Christ endured the cross, despising the shame. His calling was to suffer these things and to enter into his glory.

He suffered, therefore, with royal dignity. His very silence was majestic. Herod, Pilate, the Roman soldiers, the Golgotha crowds — none of these with cajoling or threats or scourging or taunting could overthrow his meekness. They, not he, became contemptible.

This is the royal suffering Peter saw; this is the example Christ left that we might follow in his steps. Peter uses a graphic word: "example" means a writing model for a pupil to trace, a "dot-to-dot" guide for the learner. Peter could not forget the glance of the sinless, guileless Sufferer, who sought no revenge but committed himself to God's righteous judgment (I Pet. 2:22, 23).

Until we are ready to follow in the steps of that Saviour, discussions of Christian vocation are futile. Had vocational counselors interviewed Simon Peter, they would likely have directed him away from the fishing business. His gifts for leadership were wasted in a two-man fishing boat. But they would hardly have recommended a career in sectarian religious extremism, as a follower of the Nazarene. Devotion to such a cause could, and did, end in crucifixion.

From the twelve apostles to the Auca missionaries of our generation, the history of the Christian church is the history of "wasted" lives. The Christian may tabulate all the assets of his personality and take inventory of his preferences, but he casts all these at the feet of Christ. He is not seeking fulfillment but expendability. He counts not his life dear to himself, for he holds it in trust for Christ. His goal is beyond the grave; the crown of his high calling is in the hand of his risen Lord.

Yet the calling of the cross is not a calling to destruction, abandonment, and frustration. Christ went to the cross only when the Father's hour had come and when his public ministry was finished. Our calling, too, has purpose and sets a task to be fulfilled.

The task is the task of the kingdom. Service in Christ's steps must be service in his kingdom. It remains a calling of the cross because the kingdom of Christ has not yet come in glory. When Jesus began his public ministry, he continued the proclamation of his forerunner John the Baptist: "The time is fulfilled, and the kingdom of God is at hand: repent ye and believe the gospel" (Mark 1:15).

The Old Testament promises had joined the coming of God's righteous rule with the coming of the Messiah. The prophets, of course, recognized God's sovereignty over all things as the Creator of heaven and earth and the Lord of history. But they proclaimed the appearing of God's saving power in a great climax of redemption. Isaiah pictured this by using the figure of the year of jubilee. The sacred calendar of the people of God was structured in a pattern of sevens: the seventh day was holy, the seventh month a time for a holy feast, and the seventh year a sabbatical. When seven sevens of years had passed, the law provided for a fiftieth year of restoration and release. Debts were canceled, prisoners freed, and every man restored to his own inheritance in Israel. Isaiah pictures the final salvation in these terms (Isa. 61:1-3). The acceptable year of the Lord will be proclaimed by the Lord's Anointed. He will bind up the broken-hearted, proclaim liberty to the captives and the opening of prison to the bound.

When Jesus came to the synagogue of Nazareth, he preached an astonishing sermon on this text from Isaiah. He declared to those among whom he had been brought up: "To-day hath this scripture been fulfilled in your ears" (Luke 4:21).

Because the time was fulfilled and the Lord had come, the trumpet of jubilee could be sounded. The kingdom had come because the King had come. Christ could cast out demons in the power of the kingdom because he had first overcome the strong man, Satan (Matt. 12:28). His disciples could no longer fast as John's had done because the Bridegroom himself was with them, and in his presence the great feast of the kingdom must begin (Matt. 9:15). Because all things were ready and the feast was spread, the Servant must now bid men to come in to the feast and not to delay or make excuse (Luke 14:17).

Yet John, the forerunner, was in an agony of confusion. He had prepared in the desert a spiritual highway for the coming Lord, promising the coming of One whose shoes he was unworthy to bear. He had declared that the axe of God's judgment was lying at the root of every tree. When the Coming One came, he would baptize with fire (Matt. 3:10-12).

But John was in Herod's prison; there he heard news of the miracles of healing being wrought by Christ. If this was indeed the Christ, why did he not lift the axe of judgment? How could the blessings of the kingdom come without the judgment of the kingdom? Can the acceptable year of the Lord begin without the day of vengeance of our God (Isa. 61:2; Luke 4:19)?

John sent messengers to Jesus with his tormenting question: "Art thou he that cometh or look we for another?" (Matt. 11:3).

Jesus kept John's disciples near him to witness his mighty works of healing and sent them back with a de-

16

scription of these miracles that would assure John of the fulfillment of the prophetic promise.

The marvel of God's grace was almost more than one preacher of the kingdom could bear. Yet if the axe of judgment had been wielded by Christ as John had anticipated, no one could have been spared, for all have sinned. God sent forth his Son in the fullness of time to bear the stroke of judgment rather than to inflict it. The saving power of God's kingdom of grace must be revealed before the coming of the kingdom judgment.

Or to put the matter in terms of the work of the King, Christ came the first time to give his life a ransom for many, but he will come the second time to exercise that universal judgment given him by the Father. In the interval, the gospel of his redeeming mercy must be carried to the ends of the earth. To this end the risen Lord sends from the throne of heaven the Holy Spirit.

In short, the call of Christ comes in this time of his kingdom while his longsuffering is waiting and while men are being gathered in from the byways of the world to God's feast. Christ has entered his glory, but he calls on us to share his sufferings. We cannot suffer in the place of others to bear their sins, but we must suffer for the sake of others, for all those who will form the church of Christ, his body.

Paul puts the matter briefly enough: "For though I was free from all men, I brought myself under bondage to all, that I might gain the more" (I Cor. 9:19). There is no slavishness in Paul's humility, no servility, only consuming purpose. Paul lives as one upon whom the ends of the ages are come.

As the writer to the Hebrews says, "For we have not here an abiding city, but we seek after the city which is to come" (Heb. 13:14). The kingdom of heaven gives its own perspective to the calling of the Christian. He is

17

a stranger and pilgrim in the city of men; he goes forth outside the camp, bearing Christ's reproach.

Just because Christ's kingdom demands absolute commitment, the disciple must hear the call, "Come ye out from among them, and be ye separate, saith the Lord, and touch no unclean thing; and I will receive you, and will be to you a Father, and ye shall be to me sons and daughters, said the Lord Almighty" (II Cor. 6:17, 18).

The city of man requires idolatry. All must bow before the symbol of its total claim. Religion is tolerated when it supports the claims of the state, the party, the institutional hierarchy. But those who say, "We must obey God rather than men" are always condemned as traitors or exiled as aliens.

Yet the calling of Christ's kingdom not only separates a man from the world, it also sends him to the world. In this time of the kingdom we are pilgrims, for the mountain of Christ's rule is the heavenly Zion; but in the task of the kingdom we are ambassadors, for we have been sent by the King to proclaim his terms of peace to his rebellious realm.

The "Come!" of Christ separates us from the world to his name; the "Go!" of Christ sends us to the world in his name.

Both commands have been isolated and misunderstood in the history of the church. Saint Anthony fled from the world to find salvation in desert solitude. When his fame made his retreat a colony, the pattern of a monastic community had been established. Through the centuries, the methods of Christian withdrawal have varied, but the motif has remained. Its fatal symptom is the withering of missionary service. Disengagement from the world denies the missionary calling of the church.

The comfortable fallacy that world-flight is peculiar to monasteries can lull us in our own van Winkle slumbers.

18

It is quite untrue, of course. Monastic missionaries wrote the history of Roman Catholic missionary expansion; on the other hand, a community of evangelical missionaries may go bravely to the field only to take refuge behind the walls of a compound. And what of the new churches of suburbia? From what have they fled? What purpose does their imaginative architecture serve?

Evidently the "Go!" of Christ may be avoided in the most ecclesiastical surroundings, with the most elaborate programs. Even mission study groups and missionary rallies may serve as excuses for sitting together instead of going to work.

And the remedy? The best-advertised cure is drastic. Let the church "get lost" in the world. The church should lose its form and find a new shape, the shape of the world. Instead of discussing irrelevant themes in archaic language, it must let the world write the agenda and enter a dialogue in earthly, or perhaps earthy, language. Cell groups where men live and work should replace solemn assemblies in the suburbs. A secular age must be penetrated by a "religionless" Christianity.

Is this cure too "worldly"? Surely not, in its bold assertion of the outreach of the church: the kingdom is a leaven penetrating all the worlds of man. But sadly so, in its confused surrender of the distinctiveness of the church: the church is called to be a light as well as a leaven, and that calling places it on a lampstand.

To identify the church with the world on the assumption that all men share Christ's salvation is to destroy the missionary calling of the church. The kingdom of light and the power of darkness, Christ and Belial, have nothing in common. Salvation means being delivered from the power of darkness and being brought into the kingdom of the Son of God's love (Col. 1:13). Christians are called to be "children of God without blemish in the midst of a crooked and perverse generation, among whom ye are seen as lights in the world, holding forth the word of life" (Phil. 2:15, 16).

The calling of the church is not just to service in the world. It is to fellowship with God, and before God. As a kingdom of priests and a holy nation, it declares the praises of him who called it from darkness to his marvelous light (I Pet. 2:9).

The calling of the kingdom, then, is the power of God that brings us from darkness into light and sets us as lights in the darkness. To seek first the kingdom of God means to seek first the purpose of God's saving rule in Christ. Seeking the kingdom is not a pious attitude that can link with any activity whatever. It is selective, re-strictive, focused action. Paul likens it to military service. The soldier on service may not become involved in other pursuits; he is under orders. Seeking the kingdom con-trasts with seeking the objectives of the world: food, clothing, shelter. Our heavenly Father knows our needs and will supply them, but building bigger barns to store surplus crops for our own ease and security is not seeking the kingdom of God; it is worldly folly, the service of mammon.

The distinction commonly made between secular pur-suits and Christian service comes dangerously close to the distinction between what the Gentiles seek and what the children of the kingdom seek. Christian calling cannot be secular. The man who hesitates between a money-making career and the ministry is not merely in doubt about his calling to the pastorate, he is questioning his commitment to Christ.

Kingdom service may include agrictulture, industry, or art; but only as such labor is done with a view to the purposes of the kingdom. Again, the calling of God is decisive. Since the program of God's kingdom requires a

20

period of time between the first and second comings of Christ, the expectation of the kingdom to come does not call for the abandonment of God's command to subdue the earth. When certain Thessalonians quit work to await Christ's return, Paul commanded them in Christ's name to work with quietness and eat their own bread (II Thess. 3:12). Only in this way can they fulfill their kingdom calling not to be weary in welldoing (v. 13). The "welldoing" of which Paul speaks is described more fully in Galatians 6:9, 10. It refers particularly to supporting the work of the gospel financially and providing for those in need both within the church and outside of it.

Kingdom service, then, includes cultural development in Christ's name, but always in the perspective of the kingdom. Every calling becomes a calling of service: service to Christ, even when a slave toils for a heathen master (Col. 3:22-24); service to men in Christ's name both in the work we do and the money we earn (Eph. 4:28).

The Lordship of Christ over all things means that every calling that serves men's needs can be Christ's calling. Conversion to Christ need not mean an immediate change of jobs or social status. The path of obedience begins where the Christian stands, and Paul exhorts the Corinthians to stick to the positions in which God called them and glorify Christ there (I Cor. 7:17-24). Any "calling"—in slavery or freedom, circumcision or uncircumcision, marriage or bachelorhood — is transformed by Christ's Lordship and becomes his calling to daily service.

On the other hand, Christ's Lordship directs the lives of his disciples, and the way of the cross requires the willing abandonment of any vocation for the sake of the Lord. In the background of New Testament history, we catch repeated glimpses of Christians who were serving

Christ as "fellow-workers." Mary Magdalene, Joanna, and Susanna provided for the needs of Christ and his disciples (Luke 8:2, 3); Dorcas sewed for the poor (Acts 9:39); Aquila and Priscilla provided hospitality for the Apostle Paul and other Christian teachers, and joined in both tent-making and evangelism; unnumbered and unnamed Christians ministered to those in prison, cared for the sick, fed the hungry, instructed the young, or interrupted business trips to imitate the Good Samaritan toward some victim of disaster. Through such vocations no less than through the apostolic preaching, the gospel was carried beyond the bounds of the Roman Empire in the first Christian century.

What are the demands of service in Christ's kingdom today?

The kingdom perspective has not changed. Christ is Lord at the Father's right hand, the present and future King.

The world has not changed, either—in its revolutionary ferment or in its hostility to the kingdom of God. Yet the opportunities have changed.

Technology has halved the time necessary to earn one's daily bread. Leisure time is kingdom time, and it is possible for a man's fullest vocation to be his avocation. The weariness we are spared by labor-saving devices must be earned in welldoing. If a fully equipped kitchen makes entertaining easier, Christian hospitality can be expanded.

Mobility is another result of modern technology. Freedom to move is freedom to serve. In what residence can your service be most effective? What about employment? American society is unique in the flexibility of job opportunities. The job you take is under Christ's Lordship. In what way does it honor him? Automation has not yet removed drudgery and monotony from industrial

22

processes. Useful work is often mechanical; it is not therefore secular. A Christian girl worked as an inspector of rubber products. She spent hours at a table with other women rapidly picking up surgical gloves, spinning them from the wrist to inflate them, and then squeezing each finger to reveal flaws or punctures. The work was necessary: flawed gloves could mean infection in surgical use. It was also monotonous. She found that her real job was more challenging: to participate as a Christian in the endless conversation of the women kept at the table by their weary task.

There are jobs that a Christian ought not to take because they serve purposes opposed to the kingdom; there are jobs that he ought not to keep when positions affording greater kingdom service are open to him; there are jobs that he ought to seek, where his skills can render particular service to the kingdom.

An able layout artist had a remunerative position with an advertising agency and contacts for free-lance work in his area. He resigned his job and moved to another city to work for the publishing house of his church. His income is lower, but his layouts now attract readers to the message of the gospel. He doesn't speak of sacrifice.

An illustrator was art director of a large art agency. His income was good; his talents seemed well used. Yet he was dissatisfied. He completed further graduate study and took a teaching position on a university faculty. His concern for other people can now find direct expression; his teaching can probe the philosophy of art and point to the realities of faith. In the perspective of the kingdom, his choice was in the direction of fulfilling his calling.

In the greater job choice possible in our society, more jobs appear with special implications for the kingdom. Mass media of communication, education, government, social service, public relations—these expanding areas indicate a shift in Western economy from the production of goods to the offering of services, from making things to helping people. Christian alertness to the kingdom imperatives must respond to these opportunities and demonstrate the transforming power of the gospel in human relations.

Nor is it sufficient for individual Christians to find their calling in such forms of service. Christians have collective responsibility to manifest in specifically Christian enterprises what the gospel means in contemporary life. The full Christian witness in education cannot be brought by the courageous efforts of isolated teachers laboring under the increasing restrictions of a secularized public school system. There must be Christian schools to provide education with the heart left in, where techniques do not become technology nor the humanities humanism.

In the other areas, too, groups of Christians must bear distinctive witness; Christian book publishing and journalism, radio, television, professional and labor associations are all opportunities that can be developed only by joint fulfillment of kingdom calling.

To be sure, there are dangers. Because Christ alone is Lord, and because he has not come in judgment, he does not now put a sword in the hands of his servants to bring in his kingdom by force. No holy wars may be fought to bring in his kingdom; it is not a kingdom of this world for which his servants may fight (John 18:36). Neither may economic force or political pressure be used as a means of fulfilling the prayer, "Thy kingdom come!"

A further danger of corporate Christian action is that the program of the kingdom may be forgotten, and the "Go!" of Christ's calling ignored. Christian villages, towns, retirement communities, year-round conference centers and the like may serve to demonstrate Christian solutions to social problems, but they cannot long flourish, for they are centers of withdrawal; Christ did not pray that his disciples should be taken from the world, but that they should be kept from evil (John 17:15). If the leaven stops working, the light is soon extinguished.

We are not now called to build the kingdom of glory, but to carry a cross in the kingdom of grace. To forget the cause of missions is to forget the purpose of Christ in a world still spared from destruction. The purpose of your life must be the purpose of Christ's death.

What your hands make, what your money buys, what your heart desires—in these you live; in these Christ calls you to gather with him those for whom he died. Because his name is written on all that you are and have, all must serve his purpose. Measure your discipleship by the things you have time for.

Gehazi, the man of God, was a disciple to Elisha. He loved the good things of life: money, clothes, property, servants. When the prophet refused an honorarium from Naaman the healed leper, it was too much for Gehazi. He followed the departing Gentile and gave him opportunity to express his gratitude by a gift for theological education (II Kings 5:21f.).

Gehazi received Naaman's gift—and his leprosy. But had not God promised blessing to his people? Vineyards, oliveyards, sheep and oxen, the very things Gehazi desired? Had not God promised that grateful Gentiles would bring their tribute to the people of God? Could not sons of the prophets, as workmen worthy of their hire, share in such largess?

Hear Elisha's rebuke: "Is it a time to receive money, and to receive garments, and oliveyards, and vineyards, and sheep, and oxen, and menservants, and maidservants" (II Kings 5:26)?

Gehazi thought there was no time like the present. The urgency of God's kingdom meant nothing to him.

25

If the service of Elisha was so urgent, what of the service of Christ?

B. CALLING FROM THE THRONE

Faced with the calling of the cross, the demand of seeking first the kingdom, every Christian must cry, "Who is sufficient for these things?" (II Cor. 2:16). The answer Paul gives we must also claim: "Our sufficiency is from God" (II Cor. 3:5).

Christ who calls us to take up the cross has ascended into heaven, and from his glory as Lord, he sends forth the royal gift of his Holy Spirit. Our service is shaped not only by the perspective of his kingdom, but also by the richness of his gifts.

1. ENDUEMENT SHAPES SERVICE

In the Epistle to the Ephesians, Paul reflects with inspired wisdom on the calling of Christ. In the fourth chapter, he deals again with a theme he had discussed in writing to the Corinthians: the unity and diversity of the work of the Spirit in the church. To walk worthily of the calling with which they are called, Christians must keep the unity of the Spirit in the bond of peace: there is one body, one Spirit, and one hope of our calling.

"But unto each one of us was the grace given according to the measure of the gift of Christ. Wherefore he saith, When he ascended on high, he led captivity captive, and gave gifts unto men" (Eph. 4:7, 8).

The one ascended Lord, through the one Spirit sent from heaven, bestows many gifts on men. The variety of these gifts does not divide, but unites the church of Christ. Indeed, Paul can speak of them not only as "gifts" but as "measures," varying amounts of the one gift of the Spirit.

Paul sees Christ's ascension in the beautiful imagery of Psalm 68. The Lord marches from the wilderness at the head of his redeemed people, and ascends into the holy hill of his dwelling and rule. As the triumphant King, he receives the fruits of his victory and distributes his largess among his people. The gift of the Spirit at Pentecost fills Christ's church with the power of his kingdom.

This presence of the Spirit both empowers and shapes the service of the church. The one body grows "according to the working *in measure* of each several part" (Eph. 4:16). The grace given in measure (v. 7) produces a working in measure (v. 16). That is, the calling of an individual in the church of Christ is determined by the gifts Christ has given him, by the "measure" of the Spirit he has received.

The equivalence of "calling" and "grace given" appears especially in the way Paul speaks of his own apostleship. He says, "But I write the more boldly unto you in some measure . . . because of the grace that was given me of God, that I should be a minister of Christ Jesus unto the Gentiles" (Rom. 15:15, 16). Again and again he describes his office and authority with this phrase (Rom. 12:3; I Cor. 3:10; 15:10; Gal. 2:9; Eph. 3:2, 7).

Paul knew that he was unworthy to be an apostle, having persecuted the church; yet his reply to his critics was that "by the grace of God I am what I am: and his grace which was bestowed upon me was not found vain; but I labored more abundantly than they all: yet not I, but the grace of God which was with me" (I Cor. 15:10).

James, Peter, and John in the church at Jerusalem recognized Paul's apostleship to the Gentiles when they perceived the grace that was given to him (Gal. 2:9). The presence of the gifts for this work attested Christ's calling to the work, for the one Spirit "wrought for Peter unto the apostleship of the circumcision" and for Paul the apostleship to the Gentiles.

27

All Christian calling is by the inward gift of God's grace as well as by the outward summons of his revealed will. Paul, called to be an apostle by the grace given him, writes to the Corinthians, called to be saints, and thanks God "for the grace of God which was given you in Christ Jesus" (I Cor. 1:4).

God's sanctifying grace brings us to the realization of our calling: "Faithful is he that calleth you, who will also do it" (I Thess. 5:24). "God is faithful, through whom ye were called into the fellowship of his Son Jesus Christ our Lord" (I Cor. 1:9).

Your personal calling as a Christian is the outworking of the measure of the gift of God's grace that has been given to you. A man ought not to think of himself too highly, but should "think soberly, according as God hath dealt to each man a measure of faith" (Rom. 12:3). As the one Spirit divided into tongues of flame to rest upon the disciples at Pentecost, so now the Lord deals (divides) to each man a measure of faith. These gifts must be exercised, and in their exercise the calling of the Christian is determined. Paul goes on to describe the gifts that differ "according to the grace that was given to us" and their corresponding functions (vv. 6-8). The man who has the gift of prophecy is to exercise it according to his measure of faith (or grace); the gift of cheerfulness finds expression in the work of benevolence.

The measure of gift also determines the measure of ministry. Paul would not glory beyond his measure in asserting his apostolic authority, but "according to the measure of the province which God apportioned to us as a measure, to reach even unto you" II Cor. 10:13).

Your sphere of action, your ministry in the service of Christ, is marked out by the gifts Christ has given you. The gifts of Christ's grace are like a majestic stained-glass window in his church. Each Christian is set in

28

place like a piece of jeweled glass, so that the radiance of God's grace may shine through him to add a beam of crimson or emerald or azure to the orchestration of color blazing within. "According as each hath received a gift, ministering it among yourselves, as good stewards of the manifold (many-colored) grace of God" (I Pet. 4:10).

Paul uses the figure of the body to stress the great diversity of these individual ministries. Seeing is quite different from smelling, and hearing from walking. Clearly the member serves best who does heartily what he is given to do as a good steward of the grace committed to him. There are no useless gifts of grace; there is no Christian without a ministry—the capacity to serve Christ and the opportunity to do it.

To be sure, there are groupings of gifts. Some Christians may be described as pastors or teachers, some as governors or rulers, some as ministers of mercy. Paul gives several lists of gifts and functions in the church (I Cor. 12:8-10, 28-30; Rom. 12:6-8; Eph. 4:11). There is particular need for grouping functions in the church which require public recognition for their proper exercise. Such functions are sometimes called "offices."

Yet even within such groupings the individual characteristics of each servant of Christ remain. Samson was one of many judges of Israel. With other judges he was given gifts of leadership for the deliverance of the people of God from their enemies. But his distinctive calling as judge was marked out by the Spirit's gift of invincible physical strength. This gift was not arbitrarily or uselessly granted. Samson was called in a time when disunity, fear, and hopelessness made the divided tribes of Israel ready prey to the power of the Philistine invaders. Samson's gift demonstrated that God was able to deliver not only by a few warriors (Gideon's three hundred), but even by one.

29

That lesson was of supreme value for the future, for the final Saviour and Judge of Israel must be One. When Samson, bound by his people and delivered up to the will of his enemies, triumphed at Lehi (Judg. 15), his unique calling became apparent. Not even David's conquest of Goliath pictured more vividly the role of Christ as the Champion and Mighty One.

Sadly, Samson's history traced the progressive quenching of the gifts of the Spirit rather than a faithful stewardship of them. Only in his death was he restored again as the deliverer and judge of his people.

Good stewardship requires a man to "stir up" the gift of God that is in him (II Tim. 1:6), as Paul charged Timothy. Only in that way will he fulfill his ministry (II Tim. 4:5). An unfulfilled ministry is an indebtedness: to God, and to those whom it might serve. Because of the grace given him as Apostle to the Gentiles, Paul regarded himself as a "debtor both to Greeks and to Barbarians, both to the wise and to the foolish" (Rom. 1:14). His preaching of the gospel was out of a necessity laid upon him by that very stewardship of grace (I Cor. 9:16, 17).

Every gift you have received, then, is a calling of the Spirit. You dare not ignore your gifts, neglect them, or wrap them in a napkin to be presented unused to Christ on his return (Luke 19:20). Indeed, you ought not even to be content with the gifts that you have, but covet more. God's giving and calling are dynamically related. When he gives, he calls; when he calls, he gives. Timothy was called by prophecy to the work of the ministry and granted further gifts at the time of his ordination (I Tim. 4:14; Tim. 1:6). Your desire to serve God more fully may be the foretaste of richer gifts equipping you for that service. It is quite possible to overestimate the gifts you have; it is quite impossible to over-supplicate the gifts you need. Your heavenly Father will not give a stone for bread or a serpent for fish; he will give the Holy Spirit to those who ask him (Luke 11:13). Our spiritual poverty can be remedied: we have not because we ask not (James 4:2).

At the same time our petitions must seek God's kingdom and not our glory. Not those gifts that most distinguish us as individuals, but those which most distinguish us as Christians must be our constant desire. The Corinthians preferred the more showy gifts, notably the gift of tongues. Paul taught them to value the gifts of the Spirit in spiritual terms. Gifts that built the church of Christ were the gifts Paul wanted. Better five words of solid teaching than ten thousand of fruitless exhibition (I Cor. 14:19). The greater gifts of teaching are less spectacular, but they build up the church, and they are to be desired earnestly (I Cor. 12:31; 14:1). Still more important are the abiding gifts on which all others rest: faith, hope, and love. These are not the gifts in which Christians differ, but they are those in which they should seek to excell. Most excellent of all is the gift of love, without which any other gift is useless (I Cor. 13). Diversities of gifts, for all of their distinctiveness and individual character, cannot lead to pride. "For who maketh thee to differ? And what hast thou that thou didst not receive? But if thou didst receive it, why dost thou glory as if thou hadst not received it?" (I Cor. 4:7).

To whom much is given, of him shall much be required (Luke 12:48). The understanding that Peter received, not through flesh and blood but by revelation of the Father, made him the more responsible as a steward of the kingdom.

2. Fellowship Shapes Service

Some athletic skills can be developed in solo practice; there are gifts of the Spirit, too, that can be exercised by one man in the presence of God. But God does not call many kicking specialists to sit on the bench until the try for an extra point. His players stay in the game, and they must work together. Your service of God is shaped not only by the gifts you have, but by the fellowship in which those gifts are used.

The word "fellowship" has become a little battered, like the furniture in the Fellowship Hall where the Men's Fellowship holds Fellowship Suppers. In the Bible it means more than camaraderie, or even comradeship. Most often it has an active sense of *sharing* together. Furthermore, it is our fellowship with God that is of first importance. The gifts of the Spirit are ours through the presence of the Spirit; to share the gift is to share the Giver in the delight of personal communion. Every gift becomes a means of worship as well as a cause for thanksgiving. The cheerfulness God gives for the service of Christian mercy is first joy before God. Yet it cannot be fully rendered back to God until it has been directed to men. God loves a cheerful *giver*. "Inasmuch as ye have done it unto one of the least of these my brethren, ye have done it unto me" (Matt. 25:40).

Within the church of Christ, the mutual ministry of gifts moves constantly to the pulse-beat of the life of the Spirit. The body grows through the organic interpedendence of each part. From the one Head, Christ, all the body "fitly framed and knit together through that which every joint supplieth, according to the working in due measure of each several part, " builds itself up in love (Eph. 4:16).

That means that you cannot grow without ministering to others and receiving the ministry of others. Try to recall the people who have stimulated your own Christian growth. In five minutes time you might name scores of people whose influence was of critical help in winning you to Christ and helping you to grow as a Christian.

If you have been growing, however, you have also been serving. You do not know all those you have served, just as you do not know all who have served you, but can you name some of them?

Failure to recognize that Christians grow together as they minister to one another can lead to painful symptoms in the body of Christ. Paul pictures the absurdity of both envy and pride among the members of the one body. A foot cannot resign from the body because it is not the hand; neither can the head say to the feet, "I have no need of you" (I Cor. 12:15, 21).

How ready Christians have been to divide the church into Seeing Eye or Hearing Ear societies, judging the usefulness of all Christian graces by the measure of their own! Fortunately for sectarian Christians, their own bodies are not dismembered by such strife; not only has God "tempered the body together" for harmonious functioning, but men support this harmony in the attention and honor they give to the less necessary parts of the body. Hair, for example, must be placed almost last in functional ranking of the parts of the body, but it is an all-time winner in awarded honors. Retiring kidneys and glamorous fingernails are joined in the one body; what the hidden organs lack in splendor they gain in importance.

Apply this spiritual physiology to the uses of Christian fellowship and you can only rejoice that Jack Shoals was made chairman of the campaign committee. Perhaps his talents *are* the most modest: he needs a little more honor for that very reason.

By the same analogy, you may need rather different Christian friends besides those you have cultivated. Who are the members of your group? Are ages and interests similar? Do you find genuine fellowship with elderly people? Are your moppet friends in short supply? There is a disturbing possibility that you may need most the spiritual gifts of Christians least like yourself in age, social background, race—even denominational affiliation.

You cannot bring your gifts to mature function apart from the mutual ministries of Christ's church. Therefore no Christian can determine his calling in isolation from the throbbing organism in which he is called. No doubt a Christian who is joined to Christ can exist outside the fellowship of the church, almost as a surgically removed bodily organ may be kept alive if the links of arteries and nerves are unsevered. But a living brain on a laboratory stand is a monstrosity. There are emergencies which may require surgery: Christians may be forced to separation, and Christ himself warned of the necessity of cutting off an offending member of the body (Matt. 18:7-9, 17). But the Christian is endued of his Lord for corporate life. His freedom and growth are found in fellowship.

No Spiritual Inventory Test can measure your gifts and capacities in Christ's service. Such a test may help you not to think of yourself more highly than you ought to think; it may reveal unsuspected abilities and strengths. But Christ's own test is not the S.I.T.; it is administered only in action. We might call it the Service In Fellowshp Test. As you labor with other Christians, hidden gifts are brought to light and new gifts are received.

3. Opportunity Shapes Service

William Carey had his own gifts of the Holy Spirit; he exercised them in a fellowship of prayer and service as pastor of a little church in Moulton. Had there been no other factor we may suppose that you would not have heard the name of this self-educated village preacher. He was a fine Christian and a poor shoemaker.

The other factor was the vision by which Carey discerned a vast opportunity. You may recall that he loved the world of God's creation and that he was a naturalist,

34

self-taught in field observation. To such a man the appeal of Captain Cook's voyages was irresistible. Somewhat to the detriment of his cobbling, he read avidly the accounts of Cook's explorations. Many other Englishmen did the same thing; they saw new worlds for commerce, new horizons for adventure or escape. Carey saw what they missed, for his perspective was that of the kingdom of God. He saw people: countless thousands of tribes and tongues around the world who had no knowledge of the gospel.

That vision of opportunity shaped Carey's life, and through him the mission of the church in a global age.

Perhaps "vision" is a misleading term to describe Carey's perception; not that it is too grand or sweeping or inclusive, but just that it sounds too easy. Carey fought for it: first in his own mind, then among his Christian friends, whose sincerely mistaken theology saw missions as a Divine act but not a Divine calling.

Every conceivable obstacle seemed to block Carey's obedience: objections from his friends, the reluctance of his wife, her long illness and death, the powerful and planned opposition of the East India company, the disinterest of those whom he sought at such vast sacrifice to reach.

Carey's opportunity rather resembled Samson's as he was delivered bound to the Philistines at Lehi. But he had the same source of strength and drank from the same spring of refreshment. The opportunity was there and Carey grasped it.

Seizing God-given opportunity counts for much in the fulfillment of your calling. Paul exhorts us to redeem the time for the days are evil (Eph. 5:16).

God is the Lord of time and Christ the King of the ages. God does not appoint a meaningless succession as the structure of our lives. Watching the clock is poor

35

stewardship on many counts. The monotonous ticking of a clock, or the steady whir of its electric motor, gives a most misleading understanding of the time of our lives. The rhythms of our bodies serve the purpose far better. Our time is measured by our waking and sleeping, our breathing in rest or our gasping in struggle, the measured beating or the rapid pounding of our living hearts.

God appoints our time in seasons. He gives the rain in season and sets the bow of his sovereign promise in the clouds. The seasons are set in his own power, not only in the circling times of a spinning planet, but in his purposes of redemption.

We have already noted the provisions of God's law for a sacred calendar with its sabbatical seasons, and at the climax of all the fiftieth year of jubilee.

Like the sacrifices and feasts it prescribed, this system carried in its own structure a witness to a better time, the time of the fulfillment of God's salvation. When Isaiah used the year of Jubilee to describe the time of God's deliverance, he expressed the inner meaning of this symbolism (Isa. 61:1-2).

We are called to redeem the time in the time of redemption: "At an acceptable time I hearkened unto thee, and in a day of salvation did I succor thee: behold now is the acceptable time; behold now is the day of salvation" (II Cor. 6:2).

Because, in the fullness of time, God sent forth his Son, we are to summon men to the feast in the mighty "now" of the gospel. This is the time when the Lord may be found; this is the time when his long-suffering waits and the Spirit and the Bride say "Come!" The pilgrim church journeys to the last great feast in the mount of the Lord: the feast of first-fruits has been celebrated at Pentecost; only the last harvest festival of ingathering remains.

To redeem the time of God's redemption, zeal and wisdom are needed. The vision of hope and love sees the urgency of the time. From Communist China comes the story of a student who suddenly unrolled a poster with a Scripture text in the midst of a crowded campus and began to declare the gospel message to the youth of the university. He was quickly arrested and his message silenced, but he had not been able to contain himself any longer. *Today* is the day of salvation. "The night is far spent," declares the Apostle, "and the day is at hand: let us therefore cast off the works of darkness, and let us put on the armor of light" (Rom. 13:12). This is the realization of those who "know the season," and who, like William Carey, expect great things from God and attempt great things for God.

Zeal sharpens discernment. Opportunities cannot be bought up by a sleeping steward. Jesus paints the picture of a girded servant, dressed for action, who opens the door at his master's knock whether it comes at midnight or just before dawn (Luke 12:35ff.).

Wisdom is also needed to buy up the opportunity. A little later we must examine the matter of understanding the Lord's will. One element of such understanding is a discernment of the times. The biblical wisdom ideal does not exalt abstract theoretical competence, but concrete practical relevance—the wisdom of life. A man who understands his physical climate well enough to be a reasonably accurate weather prophet, but cannot interpret the spiritual climate, is a fool (Luke 12:56).

What opportunities do you perceive? The first doors are in the room where you are. The Lord has given you a certain set of present circumstances. Paul refers to this as a man's "calling" (I Cor. 7:17). Like the heritage of an Israelite in the land, it is the "lot" or "portion" that the Lord gives you today. Here you must begin; indeed, here you must be willing to remain until other doors of opportunity are perceived and opened. The surest way to miss future opportunities is to ignore present ones. Perhaps this lesson is hardest to learn for those who are preparing for future service. Since education has gained such importance in our culture, young people often spend years being educated before any purpose in their education becomes apparent.

Meaningless course-taking becomes a way of life, more real than the vaguely conceived future, but yet not life in earnest. To conclude that the major decisions affecting the course of life must be made under such circumstances can be depressing indeed. It is heartening to remember the promises of God's faithfulness, but action is needed, too. In the student's calling, there are today's opportunities which God sets before us to prepare us for those of tomorrow. In the lonely student you befriend, the confused roommate you encourage, the article for the college paper that you write, or the Sunday School class you teach may lie the key to your future. It is in the service that you render whether in the classroom or out of it that your gifts are proved and manifested.

But *you* must seize the opportunity in the soberness of wisdom and the zeal of love.

Part Two

WHAT IS GOD'S CALLING TO THE MINISTRY?

3.

DISTINCTIVE CALLING

We have considered Christian calling; what now of the call to the ministry? Just what is "the ministry"?

A. DISTINCTIVE IN AUTHORITY

To answer that question we must begin with Jesus Christ. A minister is a servant; Christ is the one Lord, who must rule until all his enemies are put under his feet (I Cor. 15:25; Col. 3:1). No one is called to lord it over the flock of Christ (I Pet. 5:3); no throne is set in the church but the one at God's right hand. On the other hand, every Christian, called by Christ's name, is united to Christ in glory. He sits with Christ in the heavenly places, and is called a king, a son of God in him (Eph. 2:6, I John 3:1).

Spiritual dominion by princes of the church is doubly impossible: Christ the king is with his people; his people are kings with Christ. Can any officer outrank an "ordinary" Christian who shares Christ's throne and will judge angels? (I Cor. 6:3). Christ's total rule obliterates all hierarchy. The Mediator does not need mediators (I Tim. 2:5).

No, the minister is not a prince, not even a master (Matt. 23:8-12). He is a servant. But Christ is a Servant, too. The Lord became the Servant; he came not to be ministered unto, but to minister, and to give his life a ransom for many (Matt. 20:28). His service fulfilled all the ministry to which the people of God are called, just as his sufferings bore all the judgment their rebellion deserved. The church has one Minister, one Apostle and High Priest of our confession (Heb. 3:1).

To the fellowship of his ministry Christ calls every Christian. When the apostles argued about rank in the kingdom, he offered his cup of suffering (Matt. 20:22); for patterns of ministry he gave them a basin and a towel (John 13:4-14). Every Christian, then, is called to share both the ministry of the cross and the dominion of the crown.

Because Christ has fulfilled all ministry, he is the final prophet, priest, and king of the people of God. On the Mount of transfiguration, from the glory of the cloud, God's voice spoke one great commandement: "This is my beloved Son, hear him!" (Luke 9:35).

Moses and Elijah, the greatest prophetic figures of the Old Testament, were with Jesus on the mount, but their typical and mediatorial role was no longer needed. "God who at sundry times and in divers manners spake in time past unto the fathers by the prophets hath in these last days spoken unto us by his Son. . ." (Heb. 1:1, 2).

Christ is the great High Priest as well as the final Prophet, for his was the real sacrifice, to which the shadowy rituals of slain animals dimly pointed. He ascended God's holy hill to sprinkle the eternal mercy-seat with his own blood and to make undying intercession for his people. (Heb. 7:25; 9:24). His is a royal priesthood: having himself purged our sins, he sat down on the right hand of the Majesty on high (Heb. 1:3).

From the riches of his perfect ministry Christ gives every grace to his people. The "universal priesthood of believers" is not a religious application of democracy. Every Christian has access to the heavenly holy place only because Christ is there among the lampstands, his priestly garment girded with royal gold (Rev. 1:13). The believer has no rights as prophet, priest, or king in his own name, but in Christ's calling his rights exceed those of every prophet, priest, or king of the Old Testament. There was no greater prophet than John the Baptist, but he that is least in the kingdom of heaven is greater than he: greater, that is, not in obedience or service, but in position, in calling (Matt. 11:9-11). After Christ's outpouring of his Spirit at Pentecost all the people of God are as prophets, sharing with Simon Peter in that confession of faith which is revealed not by flesh and blood, but by the Father in heaven (Matt. 16:18). In that same Spirit they are sanctified, offer themselves as living sacrifices, praise God, and make intercession for men as a kingdom of priests (I Pet. 2:9). Through the power of the risen Christ they have dominion over the hosts of darkness and will rule with Christ at his appearing (I Cor. 4:8; 6:2, 2; Rom. 16:20).

All office in the New Testament church centers in Christ. He is the one Mediator, the Lord and the Servant. Because there is one Master, all Christians are brethren (Matt. 23:8). None can stand above the others. Advancement in the kingdom is not by climbing but by kneeling. Since the Lord has become Servant of all, any special calling in his name must be a calling to humility, to service. The stairway to the ministry is not a grand staircase but a back stairwell that leads down to the servants' quarters.

To be sure, some servants are granted greater responsibilities than others, but only the unfaithful servant sees such a charge as a license to abuse his fellow-servants (Luke 12:45, 46). The true steward understands that greater responsibility means deeper service: to whom much is given, much shall be required (Luke 12:48).

Only in this way can we receive the New Testament teaching about the glory of the ministry of the gospel. Let a man choose the ministry for professional dignity, easy income, personal prestige, or public praise, and he has rejected the ministry of Christ. Paul shows us what to expect: ridicule, humiliation, persecution, heartache, while we borrow other people's troubles to make them the burdens of a pastor's love.

You will not be called to all the shame that Paul endured. The ministry to which he was called as an apostle was a greater stewardship than yours, and the humiliation was greater, too (Cor. 4:9-14; II Cor. 11:23-30).

Perhaps we are now ready to think about authority. As there are differing gifts and differing degrees of stewardship, so there are differing measures of authority granted to the ministers of Christ. This is particularly clear in the case of the apostles. Paul spoke of the authority given him by Christ for the upbuilding of the church (II Cor. 13:10). He knew that he had been called as a wise masterbuilder to build up the church upon the one Foundation, Jesus Christ (I Cor. 3:10, 11).

The stewardship of the apostles was unique. They were called to be witnesses to the words and deeds of Christ, and particularly of his resurrection. The exacting requirements of an apostle's witness are specified in connection with the choice of Matthias to take the place of Judas (Acts 1:21, 22). Peter speaks of God's selection of chosen witnesses in describing his own calling (Acts 10:41, 42). Even Paul defends his own apostleship as extraordinary because he was not a disciple of Christ during His earthly ministry. Paul was an apostle "born out of due time" but called by the risen Christ Himself (I Cor. 15:8).

The ministry of the apostles brought the word of Christ to the church and the world; they testified to the things they had seen and heard as the Spirit of Christ brought them to their remembrance (John 14:26). Their calling could not be continued in later generations, for the simple reason that it was a calling of eyewitnesses. Christ's own authority is shown in this. The apostles are not independent sources of heavenly wisdom. The word they declare is the word of Christ. They are not legislators but reporters and interpreters. They become foundation stones of the church only because Christ is the chief cornerstone (Eph. 2:20).

If the work of the apostles in laying the foundations cannot be continuous, neither can the work of building ever cease. The apostles were both eyewitnesses and ministers of the Word. Upon the foundation of the inspired apostles and prophets Christ established his church. His words and deeds were recorded, his gospel was preached. The apostolic church must ever after remain upon that foundation. But the church must grow on that foundation to become one vast temple of living stones. Faithful men who received the apostolic gospel must teach others also (II Tim. 2:2). The ministry of the Word can never cease, for it is by this ministry that the church grows (Rom. 10:14, 15; Eph. 4:11-16).

In addition to the inspired apostles and prophets, Christ also gives to his church evangelists, pastors and teachers (Eph. 4:11). Such men are called to preach the Word with authority. They do not share with the apostles in the inspiration that first delivered Christ's gospel, but they do share in the stewardship that ministers it.

The steward of biblical times was an overseer among the servants. He carried the keys to his master's house and bore responsibility for its administration. He was a servant among fellow-servants, but with authority.

45

The authority of the steward in Christ's house is completely tied to the Word he preaches. When Simon Peter, by revelation from the Father, confessed that Jesus was the Christ, the Son of the living God, Jesus blessed him. He had been made Peter, the Rock, and upon this rock Jesus declared that he would build his church. To Peter Christ then gave the keys of the kingdom: the authority to bind and loose on earth with heavenly sanction (Matt. 16:19).

The blessing of Christ will be misunderstood if we separate Peter from his confession. It was not Peter himself who is called the Rock, but Peter the Confessor, the inspired apostle. This becomes plain when Jesus in the same passage calls Peter a stumbling-block (Matt. 16:23). Peter confessing Christ is a rock of foundation by the Father's grace; Peter urging Christ not to go to the cross is a stumblingstone, a mouthpiece of Satan.

Neither may we separate Peter from the other apostles; not only is he their spokesman, but they share the power of the keys; the description of the authority of binding and loosing is repeated in Matthew 18:18 and applied in the plural to all the apostles, indeed to the church itself.

"Binding" and "loosing" were terms applied by the rabbis both to practices and persons. The interpreters of the law who "sat in Moses seat" (Matt. 23:2) declared some practices to be under the ban, *i.e.* not permitted by the law, while others were loosed, *i.e.* permitted. As applied to persons, binding and loosing meant to declare under discipline for an offense or to restore to fellowship after repentance. This is the meaning in Matthew 18:18, where a man who will not hear the church is declared to be as a gentile or a publican, that is, as bound by church discipline.

The figure of the keys was also used in Judaism. In the non-biblical II Baruch 10:18 we read: "Moreover, ye priests, take ye the keys of the sanctuary, and cast them into the height of heaven, and give them to the Lord and say: 'guard thy house thyself, for lo! we are found false stewards.' "* As stewards of God, the priests used the keys to admit or exclude men from the house and presence of God. Jesus condemns the lawyers and scribes who took away the key of knowledge and shut the kingdom of heaven against men (Luke 11:52; Matt. 23:13).

Christ himself bears the key of the house of God (Isa. 22:22; Rev. 3:7), but he gives to his stewards the authority to declare in his name both the good news of the forgiveness of sins and the judgment that follows impenitence. When a brother has offended one of Christ's little ones and will not repent, he must be excluded from the fellowship of the church. Such action must be taken by more than one steward; but when two or more are agreed, the validity of their decision springs from the presence of Christ himself in the midst (Matt. 18:15-20).

Just as two witnesses are necessary to deal with an offending brother, so also two witnesses were sent out by Christ to preach the gospel. Both the twelve and later the seventy disciples were sent out two by two. (Mark 6:7; Luke 10:1). Here we see the authority with which they preached: when a house or a village would not receive their message, they were to shake the dust off their feet as a witness against them (Matt. 10:14; see Acts 13:51). Sandals were used as a seal of legal procedures in the Old Testament (Deut. 25:5-10), and continued to be used in Judaism as one of the insignia of the courtroom. Shaking off the dust was a solemn warning of judgment to those who refused their word.

*Translation by R. H. Charles, *The Apocrypha and Pseudepigrapha* (Oxford: Clarendon, 1913), vol. 2, p. 486.

Jesus himself preached with authority, and not as the scribes, and those sent to preach in his name must preach with authority, too. They do not go out with pious advice or moral instruction. They are heralds of the kingdom, proclaiming that eternal consequences rest upon the acceptance or rejection of their message. Upon those who receive the gospel the blessing of the Messianic peace is pronounced (Matt. 10:13). This is nothing less than the declaration of sins forgiven (John 20:21-23). Upon those who reject the kingdom their declaration of judgment is no less sure (Matt. 10:14, 15). Such preaching uses the keys of the kingdom: it sets before men the Son's revelation of the Father and becomes a savor of life unto life or of death unto death.

The authority of preaching is confirmed by the sacraments. In the Great Commission, Christ commands that the seal of baptism be used to place the name of the Father, Son, and Holy Ghost on those who are made disciples (Matt. 28:19, 20). Such baptism is more than John's preparatory cleansing in view of the coming kingdom. It signifies the blessing of the kingdom itself which is proclaimed in the gospel message. To baptize into God's name is to use the keys of the kingdom, declaring men loosed from sin in the blood of Christ (Rev. 1:5). The Lord's Supper, as the symbolical feast of the new covenant, also seals the blessing of the remission of sins. Both these sacraments symbolize what the preaching of the cross declares: "Believe on the Lord Jesus Christ, and thou shalt be saved, and thy house" (Acts 16:31).

The power of the keys does not put the steward of the gospel in Christ's place. It does not assign to fallible men the determination of God's decrees of salvation. Only the faithful declaration of God's own Word carries this authority. The message comes in Christ's name, not in the

48

preacher's. And, of course, not everything that is said or done in Christ's name has heavenly validity. Beside the promise of the keys we must place the warning of Matthew 7:22, 23. To some who preach and even work miracles in Christ's name, the Judge will say at last: "I never knew you: depart from me, ye that work iniquity."

The herald proclaims the message of the King, the steward ministers that good deposit committed to him. The authority of the minister of God's Word is purely ministerial, never imperial—ministers cannot be "lords over God's heritage" (Luke 22:24-30; I Pet. 5:3). Preaching declares God's Word, it does not legislate nor substitute the tradition of men (Mark 7:7-9). Its authority is spiritual: no physical penalties or temporal power may be wielded by the servants of Christ in his kingdom (John 18:36, 37; II Cor. 10:3-6; II Tim. 2:24-26).

That is to say, Christ's authority is the beginning and end of the authority of preaching.

A simple truth, but it is a sword with two edges. On one side it cuts down all clerical pride. The power and the glory are Christ's. The man serves him best who best reflects the humility, even the humiliation of the Master's service (Luke 22:26, 27). The best steward is servant of all.

On the other side it cuts away all rebellion against Christs' true ministers. If the authority is Christ's, it must be respected. It is Christ who gives men the gifts and responsibilities for ministering his word. He calls men to the ministry of the gospel, and makes them stewards of the mysteries of God's revelation. (I Cor. 4:1, 2). Not all Christians are apostles, neither are all Christians pastors or teachers (I Cor. 12:29; Eph. 3:2, 3; 4:11, 12).

To be sure, the gifts of a pastor or teacher are not different in kind from those granted to other Christians. The measure of pastoral gifts is a measure of faith, as

49

Paul speaks of it (Rom. 12:3). The pastor must be able to understand and communicate the Word of Truth, yet every Christian has knowledge of the truth and must be ready to exhort his brother, teach his children, and give a reason to the inquirer for the hope that is in him (Heb. 3:13; Eph. 4:29; 6:4; I Pet. 3:15). The pastor must be able to show mercy in Christ's name, to manifest the compassion of the Saviour toward the poor, the sick, the suffering. Yet no Christian lacks either gifts or responsibility for showing mercy in the name of Christ; indeed, the one who has never given a cup of cold water in Christ's name, or visited the sick and imprisoned, or clothed the friendless, or lodged the stranger,—that one has neither served Christ nor known him (Matt. 25:31-46).

There is however a significant difference in the degree of the gifts given by Christ, as well as in the degree of faithfulness with which the gifts have been exercised. Every Israelite had the gift of physical strength from God in some measure. But not every Israelite had that degree of strength given to Samson. With strength in that degree went a calling to service that others could not render.

So with the ministry of God's Word. God does call workmen in the Word with deepened insights to perceive the outlines of sound words and with anointed lips to declare them. There are men made "mighty in the Scriptures" (Acts 18:24). A stewardship of the gospel is committed to such men. They have no choice: woe is them if they preach not the gospel! (I Cor. 9:16, 17; Col. 1:25).

As they are obliged to preach, so others are obliged to hear. Their message must be received as the word of God (I Thess. 2:13); those who by faith receive their witness will rejoice in the day of Christ's return, while those that obey not the gospel will know the judgment of God's vengeance (II Thess. 1:8-10).

The congregation must respect the authority of ministers of the Word as those "over them in the Lord" (I Thess. 5:12) to be esteemed highly in love for their work's sake. "Obey them that have the rule over you, and submit yourselves: for they watch for your souls, as they that must give account, that they may do it with joy, and not with grief: for that is unprofitable for you (Heb. 13:17).

Men are placed in this office by the Holy Spirit (Acts 20:28). Christ's gifts of the Spirit and his calling in the Spirit must be recognized by the church. When the church calls a man to the gospel ministry it is recognizing and expressing the call of Christ. The church must seek out those who are "full of the Holy Ghost and wisdom" for the particular work to be committed to them (Acts 6:3). Since the scope of a man's ministry is determined by the riches of his spiritual gifts, the recognition of a man's field of service is dependent on recognition of the gifts granted him by the spirit for that area of ministry (Gal. 2:7-9).

Other ministers or the church as a whole cannot *delegate* authority to him who is to be a minister of Christ. They can only give orderly recognition to the fact that Christ has called this man. The evidence they recognize is the fruitfulness of the gifts of Christ in the life of his minister. Public recognition is necessary, for the reason that the stewardship of Christ's Word must be exercised with authority. Those who declare the way of life and use the keys of the kingdom must be heard and heeded, and this means that their gifts must be openly acknowledged and their stewardship responsibly discharged in fellowship with the whole church as well as with those who share their special gifts for rule and teaching.

B. DISTINCTIVE IN FUNCTION

The New Testament teaches that Christ calls some men to a particular ministry of the Word and that these men exercise authority in the faithful stewardship of their office. The church must acknowledge this authority as the gift of Christ. Reflection on the authority of the office of the minister of the gospel should be sobering and even alarming. No man can take up such responsibility as a mere profession. Authority alone does not define the work of the minister, however. Others beside the preacher are called to publicly recognized ministries in the church. What precisely is the calling of the minister of the Word? What particular gifts does he need to do his work?

When we turn to the New Testament to discover how the calling of the minister of the gospel is related to other callings in the church we find an abundance of information but no one brief summary. The New Testament contains no manual of church order, to the secret despair of some tidy organization men. God's Word records the *history* of redemption to the last. The truth at it is in Christ continues to unfold through the final chapter of Revelation and Christ's ordering of his church unfolds with it. To realize what the New Testament is *not* we have only to compare it with the *Manual of Discipline* of the Dead Sea sect.

But what the New Testament appears to lose in legal crispness it gains in both richness and spiritual applicability. Manuals of order must constantly be revised: the specific answers their users require have a way of changing with the times. God's Word provides us with the principles of church order in a setting that widens their applicability. The establishment and development of Christ's church is revealed in a history that traces the purpose and work of the Lord.

What we are shown in the New Testament is the dividing of the tongues of flame as the gifts of Christ filled his church. The downward rush of the Spirit's fullness equipped apostles for the establishment of the church and surrounded them with prophets and miracle-workers, healers and rulers, preachers and counselors, prudent administrators of relief funds and cheerful visitors of the afflicted. Among the teeming variety of spiritual gifts were some that had special significance for the beginning of the Christian church. As we have seen, the inspiration of the Spirit was needed to express in words given of the Spirit the revelation of the Lord to his people. Signs of the new heavens and earth were also given to mark the truth of the inspired apostolic witness and to reveal the character of the kingdom they preached.

In Paul's lists of the gifts of the Spirit these particular gifts are named along with others not directly linked with the giving and attesting of new revelation in Christ (Rom. 12:6-8; I Cor. 12:8-10; 28-30; Eph. 4:11). Yet Paul himself leads us in distinguishing among the gifts of the Spirit to stress those which are most useful for the up-building of the church (I Cor. 12:31; 13:13; 14:1-19).

During the New Testament period the closing of the apostolic age is foreshadowed. The emphasis Paul places on the orderly use of the Spirit's gifts prepares us for the time when extraordinary gifts and offices will have come to an end (I Cor. 14:32,33, 40).

The church rests upon the foundation of the apostles and prophets, but in later centuries its upbuilding must be carried forward by evangelists, pastors, and teachers. These men, like the apostles, have gifts for teaching with authority the Word of Christ. Their work is marked out from other continuing offices in the church by their concern with the explanation and application of the Word. Paul mentions gifts for rule in distinction from gifts for teaching (Rom. 12:8; I Cor. 12:28). It would appear that in the church, as in the Jewish synagogue, there were governing elders who were not recognized as official teachers of the law (I Tim. 5:17; Luke 22:66). In rebuking the Corinthians for carrying financial disputes before heathen magistrates, Paul urges them to set up their own bench of judges to handle such cases. In view of the fact that Christians are to judge angels, the least qualified should suffice to determine such petty matters as money and property! (I Cor. 6:1-4).

Still another area for continuing ministry was the church's care for human need within its fold and without. Here "ministry" came very close to its original meaning: tables had to be served and suffering relieved by Christian Levites who did not pass by on the other side.

At first the apostles ministered in each of these ways. They established the church with their teaching, governed it, and cared for the widows and orphans in Christ's name (Acts 2:42; 4:37). With the growth of the church and its needs, the apostles asked that seven men be chosen to administer the support of the poor (Acts 6:2, 3). Whether the seven were deacons in the later sense or whether their choosing marked the first differentiation of church office, so that they were both evangelists and deacons; in any case it was evident that the continuing church required officers who could give themselves to the ministry of tables. It is possible that this phrase is here used technically to describe money-tables and therefore the administration and accounting of relief funds (cf. Luke 19-23; Matt. 25:27).

Still later we read an almost casual reference in Acts to the elders at Jerusalem (Acts 11:30). The lack of any description of their office seems to imply that it was a familiar one. In his gospel, Luke has spoken of the elders at Jerusalem in reference to members of the Sanhedrin

(Luke 22:52). It appears that in the renewed people of God a similar office continued. When a critical matter of doctrine had to be determined, the apostles did not decide it by themselves, but in council with the elders (Acts 15:6). Again the procedure followed the familiar pattern of the spiritual government of Israel. How many of the elders of the church at Jerusalem were also teachers, "scribes of the kingdom" promised by Christ, (Matt. 23:34) it is impossible to say. In Jewish usage of the time the term "elder" could be used to describe all the members of the governing council, or the "lay" members in distinction from the scribes or priests (Luke 22:66).

The term "elder" continues to be used for officers in the Christian church, particularly those with gifts for teaching (I Tim. 5:17; 3:2). The title "bishop" or overseer is also used for those who are elders (Acts 20:17, 28; Phil. 1:1; I Tim. 3:1).

The interrelation of these offices in the New Testament church shows the range of gifts necessary for the minister of the gospel. Since his proclamation is with authority it cannot be separated from the discipline of the church; there can be no discipline apart from the Word, and the public ministry of the Word must use the keys of the kingdom for a faithful stewardship of the mysteries of God. The minister of the gospel must therefore be a bishop, a governor, in the church. There may be elders in the church who do not have the gift of teaching, but there cannot be teachers of the church who do not have the gift of rule. To be sure, the gift of teaching, a combination of insight into the Scripture and the ability to communicate it, does not itself include the practical judgment necessary for governing. A Christian may be an excellent teacher and theologian without the gifts for rule. But he cannot be an official teacher in the church. The public preaching and teaching necessary for the edification of the church includes authority in application to the needs of men. Such authority can be exercised only by those who have the wisdom and judgment of an elder in Christ's church.

The gifts of the deacon are also necessary for the ministry of the Word. It is significant that the term "deacon" can be used in two distinct specialized senses: to describe the ministry of mercy and the ministry of the Word (Phil. 1:1; Col. 1:7; Thess. 3:2). No service requires deeper humility than the ministry of the Word. For this reason Paul described his apostolic vocation by the title, "Slave of Jesus Christ," and declared that he was also a servant of men for Jesus' sake (II Cor. 4:5).

Indeed there are aspects of the ministry of mercy that the pastor may commit to others just as the apostles did (Acts 6:2-4), so that he may give himself to the service of the Word. Yet the minister of the Word must have the necessary gifts for the diaconate; like the deacon he must be aple to show mercy with cheerfulness and to administer funds with discretion and prudence. Both the heart of mercy and the hand of help must characterize the man who holds forth the Word of life.

Further, each of these ministries has a dimension of depth. Each is a service of God and man, of the church and the world. As directed to God immediately, "service" becomes worship; as directed to the church, service is a ministry of edification; as directed to the world, service implies mission. Since each form of ministry has this depth, and since the ministry of the Word includes the ministry of rule and of order, a dazzling spectrum of gifts and duties is the portion of the man of God.

He ministers mercy to the world: in the hospital ward he brings cheer to the stranger, on the streets of the inner city he is friend to the bitter, in his study he counsels the confused couple whose marriage is disintegrating.

He ministers mercy to the church: visiting the aged, comforting a young man on the eve of an exploratory operation, discovering the acute financial need that threatens a growing family in the wake of illness and unemployment.

He ministers mercy before the Lord in the service of worship: praying for the sick and needy with genuine compassion, dedicating the offerings of God's people with heartfelt praise.

In the ministry of order he must also serve the world, the church, and the Lord. The discipline of love purifies the church to be presented to God and presents a clear witness of holy living to the world. Unless the minister and his people "become blameless and harmless, children of God without blemish in the midst of a crooked and perverse generation," they will not be seen as lights in the world (Phil. 2:15). No pastor should despise administrative duties. They are included in his calling. A recent survey reported that most ministers resented the demands of administration upon their time. They felt they had been prepared to minister the Word and the sacraments but were delivered up to the administration of building campaigns and fellowship suppers. No doubt a corrective is needed. Sometimes the church is just too big; sometimes it is busy with the wrong programs. A pastor is not likely to be irked with the administration of a program of evangelistic calling by the members of the congregation. Sometimes the pastor is at fault for seizing leadership himself instead of cultivating it in others. But the minister who supposes that his calling is to the pulpit and the study had better dedicate an office desk to the service of the Lord.

Yet, above all, the minister must bear the Word of God in the full depth of his stewardship. With the Word he enters the presence of God as he leads public worship.

Only with the Word can men ascend God's holy hill, for God's promises are the only plea of a redeemed people. Worship is always an echo, reflecting the word of grace with the cry of praise. Preaching, too, is worship, for the naming of God's name and the proclamation of his mercy is itself an act of praise. The minister at the Lord's table or the baptismal font continues to be a minister of the Word. For this reason he administers the sacraments: not because he has a claim to a separate priesthood, but because the sacraments seal the Word and are observed as part of the proclamation of the Word to men.

The minister of the Word who stands before God also stands before men. He proclaims the Word to the world and ministers it to the church. Every minister of the Word is both evangelist and pastor. Because gifts differ, one man may be particularly blessed in reaching those outside of Christ while another may have his greatest effectiveness in instructing believers. So pronounced may be the divergence of these two ministries that the first may be called an evangelist and the second a pastor. Both men, however, are called to minister the Word as members of Christ's witnessing church. The evangelist who disregards the church is guilty of the same error as the pastor who ignores evangelism. The gospel must still be heralded even among those who know it best, and the teaching that builds saints in the faith is also used of the Spirit for the conversion of sinners. We need both evangelists and pastors but above all we need men who are both: pastoral evangelists and evangelistic pastors.

Evangelism and pastoral teaching both require personal application of God's Word; when these three elements are drawn together we have a description of preaching that includes the many terms used in the New Testament. Preaching includes the proclamation, explanation, and application of the Word of God. Proclamation differentiates preaching from many modern methods of religious communication. The pulpit is not a psychiatrist's couch or a seminar room. The preacher is a herald, an announcer, not a pollster. In the New Testament the words for preaching ring with the authority of proclamation. The principal terms are drawn from the language of public life rather than from philosophical dialogue or religious ecstasy. The preacher is a messenger of the kingdom announcing the good news of the redemption God has wrought. His word is a trumpet call: "Thus saith the Lord." He bears witness to the decisive intervention of God and calls men to a decision. The preacher does not talk in scholarly footnotes nor does he cajole men with an ingratiating whine. He stands with boldness, using free speech before God and men in the authority of heaven's messenger. Whether men hear or refuse, they must be told.

Proclamation means evangelism, but just because the news is good news the preacher stops to explain the message. He becomes a teacher as well as a herald. A second group of New Testament terms centers around this function of the preacher. The importance of teaching flows from the fact that the gospel fulfills the promises of God. In the days of promise and preparation, prophecy often had an oracular form. The Word of God came without full explanation, for so great was the promised mystery that men could not receive a full explanation of what God would do. The risen Christ was a Teacher. He explained the Scriptures to his disciples, showing them how his sufferings and the glory which should follow were foreshadowed in promise and symbol. Only in the light of the fulfillment could the whole explanation be given. The Spirit of the Risen Lord is the Teacher of the church and the preacher explains his Word.

The teacher must remember his hearers and provide milk for children and meat for adults. His instruction

59

must be orderly and progressive, lucid and graphic. His message is wisdom, knowledge, instruction; he must discuss, persuade, reason, remind.

This leads to the third aspect of preaching, reflected in yet a third group of New Testament terms: preaching means *application:* the preacher exhorts, comforts, reproves, rebukes, warns, and censures (II Tim. 3:16; 4:2; Tit. 1:9). He converses with the church in the intimate fellowship of the upper room (Acts 20:11) and admonishes them when they fall short of obedience to God. The New Testament epistles are full of such exhortations. Preaching today requires apostolic practicality as well as apostolic orthodoxy.

Laying out the spheres of the ministry in any organized way brings to light the manifold variety of service it requires. For this very reason the service itself does not remain in neat pigeon-holes. The minister who stands in the pulpit is ministering to God, the church and the world all at once; in the hospital room he brings the comfort of Christ to a dying saint and at the same time witnesses to the power of the gospel to the patient in the next bed; in a meeting with church leaders he discusses the activity calendar, mindful that his own schedule is that of a father as well as a minister. As pastor he ministers the Word not only to the congregation in worship but to the children in an instruction class, to a group meeting for Bible study in a home, to the young people in a summer camp.

C. DISTINCTIVE IN GIFTS

If this survey of the function of the minister has not given you pause, please abandon all thought of becoming a minister. If it has, be encouraged. To the degree that you are overwhelmed you show a willingness to take the ministry seriously.

But a serious question is also raised. What gifts are necessary for such a calling as this? Dare any man suppose that God is equipping him for such service?

Better and better. Paul himself cried, "Who is sufficient for these things?" Unless you share that confession your conception of the ministry is too low. Further, God gives richer graces as his steward is faithful. You do not now have all the gifts you will have when the full demands of the ministry fall upon you. And even then you will still be pressing on to lay hold on that for which you were laid hold on by Christ Jesus (Phil. 3:12).

If, however, you are not to think of yourself more highly than you ought to think, you must judge whether God is granting to you some firstfruits of his grace in those areas needed for the ministry of the gospel.

What are they?

They are all a measure of faith. A man's "natural" gifts cannot add up to a probability that he should choose the ministry. God has chosen the weak and foolish, not the mighty and wise, so that it might be quite clear that he alone is the Saviour. If you are a gifted speaker you should be effective as a lawyer or a salesman, but nothing can be said about your effectiveness as a preacher. The glib confidence of a ready tongue may be the very pride that bars you from the ministry. Not one of the apostles was an orator. If God calls you to speak for him, the speaking will be made possible. As God said to Moses when he protested his inarticulateness—"Who made man's mouth?" (Ex. 4:11).

That word of God to Moses tells us two things: all that we have, God has given; all that we need, God will give. Apart from faith nothing in us can serve God or qualify us for his choice, but by faith all that we are is consecrated to his service, and all that we shall be.

The minister's gift of faith draws him to a life of commitment to Christ. We have seen that the calling of discipleship is the calling of the cross. This must be particularly evident in the life of the minister. Examine your calling in this respect. Are you a slave of Jesus Christ, already "bound in the spirit" to go wherever he calls you? (Acts 20:22). Are you willing to leave all and follow him, to rejoice in sufferings, to become a fool for Christ's sake? (I Cor. 4:9-13).

The commitment of faith is measured by action—the ready obedience of spiritual discipline. The minister is a good soldier of Jesus Christ, trained to obey at once (II Tim. 2:3, 4), a practiced athlete (I Cor. 9:24-27), a hardworking farmer (II Tim. 2:6), a faithful steward (I Cor. 4:2). Growth in this discipline marks Christ's calling. Timothy had to be reminded by Paul that God had not given a Spirit who produced fear, but a Spirit of love, power, and discipline (II Tim. 1:7 A.R.V.).

Commitment to God also produces humility. The meekness of Christ must be the pattern of every servant who follows him (II Cor. 10:1; I Pet. 2:21-23). Only the commitment of faith bears such fruit. It is not a cringing servility that fears to condemn evil but a royal meekness that commits judgment to God and cannot fear men.

The minister's commitment of faith must be grounded in the knowledge of faith. Timothy was nurtured in words of faith and sound doctrine (I Tim. 4:6). From a child he knew the Holy Scriptures that make men wise to salvation (II Tim. 3:15). The man of God abides in what he has learned (II Tim. 3:14) and gives himself wholly to them, so that his progress may appear to all (I Tim. 4:15). Calling to the ministry and love of the Bible go together. If you do not share the privileges of Timothy's childhood you have the greater obligation to read and study the Word of God. This habit, so characteristic of Christian faith, takes most specific form in the life of one called to the gospel ministry. He gives himself to both the understanding and the practicing of Scripture. The knowledge of faith is more than a grasp of Biblical facts. It includes a living response to the Biblical message.

This results in that growth in wisdom for which the Apostle Paul so often prayed (Phil. 1:9, 10; Eph. 1:17-19; Col. 1:9, 10). Men chosen for leadership in the church of God must have spiritual wisdom. Wisdom is the fruit of applying God's revelation in Christ to the issues of daily life. It discerns the times, seizes the opportunities, perceives truth and brings error to the test. It is the fruit of spiritual maturity, but age cannot measure it. God gives wisdom to the young as well as the old. The minister of Christ must admonish every man and teach every man "in all wisdom, that we may present every man perfect in Christ" (Col. 1:28).

The commitment and wisdom of faith are in a special sense marks of the minister. In faith and love he grows in the image of Christ, and therefore in holiness. His power in the service of God must be drawn from his walk with God. To be sure, God may use the words of an ungodly preacher to reach sinners with the truth, but a hireling has no real care for the sheep, and the natural man does not understand the things of the Spirit of God (John 10:2; I Cor. 2:14). Power for service is the work of the Spirit, and God gives the Spirit to those who ask him (Luke 11:13); Acts 4:31). The minister must be a man who has learned to walk with God in a life of prayer (Eph. 1:16).

Such a man is prepared to serve his fellow men. Love for God becomes the source of love for men. The compassion of Christian service is the compassion of Christ. What is done for the least of his brethren is done for Christ. Paul was a mother (Gal. 4:19), a father (I Cor. 4:14, 15; II Cor. 9:2), a brother (Gal. 4:12; 6:1) to those whom he served. In the agony of love he bore the burdens of the churches, and would have been willing to be accursed from Christ for the sake of his unbelieving fellow-Jews (Rom. 9:3).

This is far more than meeting people easily or enjoying social occasions. The minister must stand beside Christ as did the first disciples and see him looking at the multitudes. Until a man has that vision he is not ready for the ministry. He cannot condemn sinners until he can first weep over them. The hospitality a minister must show (I Tim. 3:2), his friendliness and gentleness (II Tim. 2:24, 25) are rooted in his desire to be all things to all men that by all means he might save some (I Cor. 9:22). The minister of Jesus Christ serves the one who was sent to seek and to save that which was lost.

The minister's love for men is exercised through particular gifts that he has for dealing with them. He must have, first, the gift of teaching (II Tim. 2:2, 24; I Tim. 3:2; Eph. 4:11; Col. 1:28, 29). We have just seen that as a man of faith he must himself abide in God's Word. But teaching is more than insight or understanding. It includes the ability to communicate spiritual truth. James warns men against too readily supposing that they have this gift (James 3:1, 2). The man who teaches must first be a hearer and then a doer of God's law of liberty (James 1:19-25).

The teacher is a workman. Like a farmer he plants and waters in God's field; like an artisan he constructs the house of God (I Cor. 3:5-15). If he uses shoddy materials—wood, hay, stubble—he may achieve a temporary effect, but his workmanship will not stand in the day of judgment. Only the endless toil of building in gold, silver, and precious stones upon the one foundation, Jesus Christ, establishes a structure that will survive the flood and the flame.

Like a householder, the teacher brings out of his treasure things new and old (Matt. 13:52). He is a scribe of the kingdom who can interpret the Word of God and pursue a right course through the Word of truth (II Tim. 2:15). He sees the "outline of sound words," discerning the great pattern of the gospel of Christ in all the Scriptures (II Tim. 1:13; Luke 24:44, 45). Through the indwelling Spirit he is a guardian of the deposit of God's truth (II Tim. 1:14). He is able to defend the truth against sophisticated attack and the antitheses of false knowledge (I Tim. 6:20).

Above all, he can apply God's Word to the needs of the hearers with all longsuffering and teaching (II Tim. 4:2). He does not engage in useless controversy but quietly and faithfully corrects the errors of those who oppose themselves (II Tim. 2:25).

He does not trim his message to please his hearers; rather he keeps back nothing that they need to know but declares to them the whole counsel of God (Acts 20:27). As Christ gave to men the words the Father gave him, so Christ's minister gives to men the words of Christ, accurately, tactfully, fully, and pointedly (John 17:8; II Tim. 4:1, 2).

A second ability is joined to teaching. The minister must be able to rule, to lead men. Here his spiritual maturity is required. The flippant, cocky adolescent should not talk too confidently of his call to the ministry. True, youth should not be despised (I Tim. 4:12—although Timothy's "youth" has been estimated at 38 years!), but youth gains respect by exemplary behavior, not by clamoring for recognition. Soberness and responsibility go together (I Tim. 3:2; II Tim. 4:5). Pastoral sobriety means alertness, watchfulness, realism. The drunk is either dead to the world or living on the moon with pink elephants. Worldly ministers are similarly nodding; they do not perceive onrushing peril; they sound no alarm to rouse the sleepers. Their split-level dreams of plenty and pleasure are illusion; not realism. Soberness is realism. Biblical soberness is not sourness or chronic depression, for it is realistic about hope, too. A skilled surgeon need not be morose; he may operate with cheerful confidence, but his face is a study in soberness.

Maturity in godliness includes much more than sober acceptance of responsibility. In word and life the minister must show love, faith, purity (I Tim. 4:12; Tit. 2:7); he is called to be an example to the people of God (I Pet. 5:3). His conduct in seeking God's glory must enable him to say with Paul: "I also please all men in all things, not seeking mine own profit, but the profit of the many, that they may be saved. Be ye imitators of me even as I also am of Christ" (I Cor. 10:33; 11:1).

The blamelessness of the minister's life is stressed in the pastoral epistles (Tit. 1:6-8; I Tim. 3:2-7). In his home and in the community, his life must witness to the cleansing power of the gospel. Men are not to be ordained to the ministry who cannot control their tongues and fists, or who love wine or money. Rather they must be righteous and devout, loving good and hating evil. Until a man is disciplined by Christ he cannot discipline others in Christ.

Finally, the maturity that is needed for leadership includes insight into men and their motives. The teacher cannot be a child, tossed about by every wind of doctrine (Eph. 4:13, 14). He must discern the wiles of the devil, unmask the pretensions of false teachers, and understand the time for stern rebuke and the time for tender entreaty. His concern must extend to young people, to boys and girls. Jesus charged Peter to feed the lambs as well as the sheep of the flock (John 21:15), and the Lord himself took children in his arms (Mark 10:16).

To become all things to all men is no small gift, but it is a necessary one for pastors. It begins with compassionate understanding, a readiness to love men where they are, for Christ's sake. The dope-addict and drunkard, the gossip and the lecher, the hypocrite and the rebel, all must be met with compassion.

This survey of the gifts and calling of the minister makes decision more difficult. Who can claim to possess such commitment to God and compassion to men, such knowledge of faith and ability to impart it, such maturity in godliness and wisdom in guiding others? Who but Jesus Christ, the great Shepherd of the sheep! He has the Spirit without measure and he gives that Spirit in full measure to the men he calls. Have you enjoyed a foretaste of those gifts?

Don't demand an answer today. You cannot program a computer to calculate your potential for Christ's ministry. You must live out the answer. Your conversation with a hitch-hiker this afternoon, your prayer for the power of God's Spirit tonight, your visit with a lonely hospital patient tomorrow, these are the stages in growth to maturity in Christ. The call to stewardship is found in stewardship. To the servant who is faithful in little the Lord entrusts much. The fruit-bearing branch is pruned for greater fruitfulness.

To *miss* your calling, follow this three-point program: assume that it begins in the future, decide that you don't know what it is, and sit down to wait for the Lord's call.

No, he has already called you—to be a Christian. Fulfill that call with all your heart and you will learn in his time what ministry is yours.

4.
CLEAR CALLING

To consider the inward call to the ministry and the outward call of the church we do not enter a screened chancel of clerical mysteries. Christ's clear call to the gospel ministry is a special instance of the way in which he calls each of his sheep by name to follow him.

Along with every believer, the minister is called to bear Christ's name, to take up his cross, and to gather men into his kingdom. This calling is intensified by special gifts that mark out his place as an evangelist, pastor, teacher. Much is given to him in the enduement of God's Spirit; much is set before him in the opportunities of God's providence; much is required of him in the fellowship of God's people.

A. YOUR PERSONAL CALLING

How, then, does Christ make clear to you your own calling in the gospel? What is his will for your life?

God has not left his will shrouded in mystery. He has spoken, plainly and fully. The man who wishes to know God's will must turn to the "oracles of God," the written revelation of the Bible. Because the Jews were given God's Word they had the "form of knowledge and of the truth." They knew God's will, approved the things that are excellent, and were made teachers of babes. (Rom. 2:17-20).

Jesus pointed men to the Scriptures and declared that they testified of him. The "word of truth" declared by the apostles showed the fulfillment of the Old Testament in Christ (Eph. 1:13; John 5:45-47). With the authority of inspiration Christ's apostles and prophets wrote the New Testament, combining truths taught of the Spirit with words given of the Spirit (I Cor. 2:13; II Peter 3:15-16).

This new Testament revelation has the finality of Christ himself. Before Christ came, revelation was incomplete. God spoke to the fathers by the prophets "at sundry times and in divers manners" (Heb. 1:1). In these last days, however, this time of fulfillment, God has spoken finally by his Son. God does not keep giving more books of the Bible because he does not keep sending Jesus Christ to die for sinners. The Bible was finished when the finished work of Christ was fully revealed. That which was spoken by the Lord Jesus was confirmed to us by them that heard him (Heb. 2:3) and the fuller revelation that awaited his resurrection was given to the apostles as Jesus had promised (John 14:25-26). Christ is the "Amen" to all the promises of God (Rom. 15:8; II Cor. 1:20).

With the final revelation in Christ the earlier ways of God's revealing his will ceased. The "sundry times" were fulfilled, the "divers manners" were taken up in the completeness of Christ's revealed glory. All that the church needs for its direction till Christ comes is given in his word, for it testifies of him.

In seeking the Lord's will, therefore, you are not in the position of Gideon who sought the sign of the fleece (Judges 6:36-40) or of David who consulted the oracular ephod of the high priest (I Sam. 23:6-12), or even of Paul who was guided at times by prophetic messages given to others or to him directly (Acts 16:6-10; 21:10-11). All these things have been written for our sakes, upon whom the ends of the ages have come, that through the patience and comfort of the Scriptures we might have hope (Rom. 15:4; I Cor. 10:11). God does not give us either Urim and Thummim or new prophecies, for the simple reason that we do not need them. The fullness of revelation has come through Christ.

There are times when we may wish that one of the old "divers manners" of revelation was still in effect. The Urim and Thummim, for example, were consulted by the priest to secure "yes" or "no" answers from God (Ex. 28:30; I Sam. 28:6). Would you be tempted to trade in the New Testament for the priest's ephod and to find your "yes" and "no" in miraculous stones rather than in Christ? In the agony of a harsh decision you might wish that this could be done. The Urim and Thummim gave infallible answers from God. One knew that success or ruin would follow a given course of action.

Could any guidance be better than that? Certainly. The guidance of Urim-Thummim was like a father's guidance of a small child. "Yes, Tim, you may go." "No, you must not do that."

The will of the father is perfectly clear, yet it may not be at all understood. It is good for a child to obey even when he does not understand. It is better for him to obey because he does understand. He must do the first to be ready for the second. The mature son understands what his father desires of him; he understands the mind of his father and his obedience is shaped by that understanding.

Without the understanding of fellowship there are difficulties in obeying an endless series of specific commands. The greatest danger is that obedience may be rendered for the wrong reasons. A man may seek to use the Urim-Thummim for magic rather than prayer. An infallible revelation of the future is a dreadful temptation to a weak sinner. God maintained his own sovereignty over the priest and the ephod by answering only at his own will (I Sam. 28:6). No man could demand of God instant revelation for every occasion.

Further, a man who does not understand may put the wrong questions or misinterpret the meaning of the answer. For example, when David inquired of the Lord concerning the success or failure of a particular military action, he was assuming that the right action was the one which would lead to success. Under the circumstances this was a justifiable assumption for David, anointed of the Lord as a warrior-king. But suppose Paul had followed the same assumption when Agabus prophesied the imprisonment he would suffer if he went up to Jerusalem? (Acts 21:10-13). His great witness before the multitudes in the temple, before the Sanhedrin, before Gentile rulers, and the emperor himself would not have been made. Paul would not have finished his course or fulfilled the calling of Christ on the road to Damascus. Paul's obedience seemed almost to be disobedience, for he was guided by an understanding of the will of Christ for his ministry that enabled him to hold fast in the face of sure suffering and even death. Like his Saviour, Paul set his face to go to Jerusalem.

Knowing the will of the Lord in the fellowship of Jesus Christ is not a technique to provide a substitute for the Urim-Thummim in securing infallible on-the-spot decisions from God. The Lord has not promised to give this, and what he does give you is far better. In his Word he reveals the principles of his will—indeed, he reveals himself. Through his Spirit he quickens your understanding of his will and your living fellowship with himself.

In Christ are hid all the treasures of wisdom and knowledge, and the Christian life means to walk in Christ

71

(Col. 2:3-6). The Word of Christ dwells richly in the heart of the Christian and produces a pure wisdom (Col. 3:16). God's will is perceived by a renewed mind, filled with the Spirit, a mind that is truly subject to the law of God, the mind of Christ (Eph. 4:23; Rom. 8:6, 7, 27; 12:2, I Cor. 2:6-16).

Paul's prayer was that Christians might be filled with the knowledge of God's will "in all spiritual wisdom and understanding" (Col. 1:9). Knowing God's will in this way means more than knowing what we ought to do; it means understanding why we ought to do it.

The Old Testament ideal of wisdom forms the background for this wisdom in Christ. The fear of the Lord is the beginning of wisdom, and it is God's wisdom that has abounded to us in the mystery of his will in the gospel (Eph. 1:9).

Wisdom is knowledge with the knower left in; or, better, it is knowledge with God left in. True knowledge begins and ends with God. The Bible never permits the split between science and religion so characteristic of the modern mind. There cannot be one kind of knowledge for understanding the world God created and another for understanding the Creator. There is meaning in creation only because God is the Creator. He is the Possessor of all knowledge and wisdom, and creation is revelation.

In the Book of Job the search for knowledge is compared to a mining operation in which men dig into the depths of the earth for hidden riches. Gold, silver, gems may be found in that way, but wisdom can be found only with God. (Job. 28:28).

In Proverbs wisdom is personified as an attendant of God, rejoicing in his works of creation, and given to men as the greatest gift (Prov. 8:22). Men should attend to God's works in nature and history as revelations of his wisdom (Ps. 19:1; 111:2, 4, 6, 10.) Yet sinners cannot

understand God's revelation in nature apart from his revealed Word. Psalm 19 joins revelation in the Word to
that in the world, and in Proverbs we read: "Every word
of God is tried: he is a shield unto them that take refuge
in him. Add thou not unto his words, lest he reprove
thee, and thou be found a liar" (Prov. 30:5).

With the revelation in Jesus Christ the true Personifi-
cation of God's wisdom is made known. The hidden
treasures of wisdom and knowledge are in him, and by
word and deed he makes known the wisdom of God.

The goal of wisdom is therefore to know Christ; to
bring every thought into his service. Such wisdom centers
where Christ is, at the right hand of God. It seeks his
kingdom, as the one treasure, the one pearl of great price.
This focus on Christ does not turn one from the world,
for Christ is the King and his power works in the world.
Nature is subject to him who walked on the waves and
ascended in the clouds. History is subject to him who has
all power in heaven and earth to bring his purposes to
pass. The Christian is subject to him in thought and in
life.

To be wise in one's own eyes, to lean on one's own
understanding is to forsake the fear of the Lord and true
wisdom. But to find wisdom in obedience to Christ joins
theory and practice in the unity of truth. Wisdom perceives God's plan and fulfills God's will.

Because wisdom applies the perspective of the revelation of God in Christ, it is not mere "practicality." The
wisdom of this world is foolishness to God, just as God's
wisdom is folly to perishing sinners. Yet wisdom is practical, ethical. It directs a man how "to walk worthily of
the Lord unto all pleasing, bearing fruit in every good
work" (Col. 1:10). For this reason Paul prays with such
eloquent urgency that Christians might be filled with
spiritual wisdom. (Col. 1:9).

Like love and joy, wisdom is "spiritual," the gift of the Spirit; indeed it is the mind of the Spirit (Rom. 8:27). The fool is filled with wine, but the wise are filled with the Spirit, and understand what the will of the Lord is (Eph. 5:15-19: Col. 3:16, 17). As love abounds more and more, the discernment of wisdom will abound with it (Phil. 1:9).

Wisdom, then, is a fruit of the Christian's walk with God as well as a guide in that walk. No Christian is perfect in wisdom. Neither does wisdom reveal God's will in the fashion of the Urim and Thummim. The Christian grows in wisdom as he grows in grace. He comes to understand better the revelation of God's Word and God's world and to discern the application of the first to the second.

Growth in knowledge and discernment enables the Christian to "approve the things that are excellent" (Phil. 1:10). This rich phrase relates our discernment to the diversities of opportunities we face. "The things that matter" (as the phrase may be translated) refers to the opportunities we should seize, the choices we should make, the things which are pleasing to the Lord (Eph. 5:10), good, acceptable, perfect in his sight (Rom. 12:2). Our "approving" or "proving" of these possibilities is a process of bringing them to the test both in thought and in life. We must prove all things, and hold fast that which is good (I Thess. 5:21).

We must prove the "times," discerning the seasons that God sets before us so that we do not act prematurely or fail to act when God's set time comes (Eph. 5:15, cf. Luke 12:56). Such evaluation enables us to redeem the time in evil days (Eph. 5:15).

We must also prove ourselves, not only as we come to the Lord's Table (I Cor. 11:28), but continually we must bring our own calling to the test (II Cor. 13:5), and

74

measure our gifts. Proving the will of God (Rom. 12:2) includes sober thinking, wise discernment as to what gifts we have received (Rom. 12:3). Such self-proving recognizes that we are being proved by God, who tests us in affliction that we may be manifested before him as those who are approved (II Cor. 8:2; Eph. 5:19, I Cor. 11:19).

In the process of proving the things that are pleasing to God we keep learning to obey his Word and to trust his hand. The two are not identical, for we must distinguish between that which God requires of us (his will in the sense of his commandments) and the mysterious providence by which he brings all his purposes to pass (his will in the sense of his sovereign decrees). When Peter tells us that it is God's will that by well-doing we should silence the ignorant charges of foolish men (I Pet. 2:15) he is speaking of the commandment of God. He then says in the next chapter, "For it is better, if the will of God should so will, that ye suffer for well-doing than for evil doing" (I Pet. 3:17). Here he is speaking of the rule of God. God's will in this sense includes the death of Christ, to which Peter refers (v. 18, see Acts 2:23), and the sufferings of Christians. We do not know as we are known; we cannot understand the mystery of God's decrees. We only know that God used the cross, the greatest crime of history, to bring redemption, and that no suffering enters our lives that does not bring with it grace now and a weight of glory in the future.

The distinction between the Word of God that we hear and the hand of God that we trust is most important for our proving of God's will. Our task is to determine what is right, not to divine what will happen. We interpret the situation by God's Word; we do not adjust God's commandments to the situation. To prove God's will means to discover how his revealed will applies to our present situation.

Do you remember the disobedience of King Saul? Samuel the prophet had not come at the appointed time; the Philistine host had camped at Micmash; Saul's army was melting away. Saul could wait no longer for the man of God. He offered the sacrifices himself, disobeying God's commandment. Was not Saul's action justified by the circumstances? So he pleaded with Samuel later; but God rejected him as king (I Sam. 13:13, 14). His action was not wisdom but foolishness.

Satan reasoned with Jesus that he should be guided by the circumstances in the wilderness. God had brought him there by the driving of the Spirit, but God had provided no food. Surely he did not intend that the Son of God should perish of hunger. Let Christ then use his power as the Son to deliver himself from suffering. Let him make the stones into bread. Christ's reply must seal our daily behavior; "It is written, Man shall not live by bread alone but by every word that proceedeth out of the mouth of God" (Matt. 4:4).

Jesus quoted the Word of God and obeyed it, and as God had cared for his people in the desert so he now cared for his Son. Angels came and ministered unto him. Living by God's Word means obeying the word of his commandment and trusting the word of his decree to deliver us at last.

Yet, while we cannot discover what is right *from* the situation, we must discover what is right *in* the situation. There are two elements in every conviction as to duty: what God's Word says and what the situation is. God's Word is infallible, but our understanding and application of it are not. The level of our spiritual maturity, our growth in grace, will affect the degree of wisdom with which we understand the application of the Word to our problems. Discernment grows with wisdom.

This ought not to dismay us, for the Lord knows our

needs. He does not permit temptations to come upon us that we cannot bear, and his hand corrects us and leads us back into the paths of righteousness, for his name's sake. Sometimes Christians speak of each decision of their lives as though they were launching a moon-shot where a single miscalculation would send the capsule into a trackless void. Even space scientists do better than that, correcting the flight of their space-probes by radioed signals. God does much better. He knows that we are often incapable of distinguishing trivial decisions from momentous ones, and that we are foolish and imperceptive. He knows—and keeps us in his hand.

There we may trust, even when we do not understand. We cannot look for certainty in every decision. If we always knew, if we always had a strong assurance that a given action was the only right course, we would not learn to trust God in the midst of suffering and darkness.

To demand complete certainty is to run grave risks: we may make our own emotional states or convictions a private Urim and Thummim, concluding that an action cannot be God's will because we do not "feel right" about it, or plunging into some enterprise because we have interpreted our own strong impulse as the Lord's leading. We must remember that the Holy Spirit sanctifies us but does not give us new revelations. Our convictions must be grounded on God's Word. We are illumined to understand it, but not inspired to write it.

This is not at all to say that feelings are unimportant. The wisdom that discerns what is pleasing to God is the believing response of the whole person, not a detached academic exercise. How often have you been surprised by your own instant reaction to a sudden situation. Only much later were you able to analyze the reasoning implicit in your response. Similarly, a sense of unease often witnesses to a violated conscience.

Joy and peace are Christ's gifts to those who seek to do his will. You may confidently thank God for these blessings as you continue in his service. They abound as God's will is discerned, and true wisdom takes account of such fruits of grace. God has not authorized us, however, to use such evidences of his goodness as a system of signals for discerning our course of action. *We* are being proved in our deeds; God is not to be proved. The child of God will yet cry with the psalmist, "Lord, why castest thou off my soul? why hidest thou thy face from me?" (Ps. 88:14). God's answer comes: "Who is among you that feareth the Lord, that obeyeth the voice of his servant, that walketh in darkness, and hath no light? let him trust in the name of the Lord, and stay upon his God" (Isa. 50:10).

We live by faith, not sight, and the pilgrim of faith sometimes must go out without knowing his immediate destination. It is enough that he journeys toward the city whose builder and maker is God. God will hear his prayer for wisdom and he will direct his steps.

How, then, in the wisdom of faith, ought you to consider your calling of Christ? One thing is clear: your calling is total. Every Christian is called to "full-time service." He must say with Paul, "To me to live is Christ" (Phil. 1:21). It is not enough to be willing to give your life to Christ, you must take up your cross and follow him. The spiritual service of every Christian is to present himself as a living sacrifice and in that total dedication to prove the acceptable will of God (Rom. 12:1, 2).

Only such dedication proves God's will in the Christian's life. But what determines the form of his service? Paul goes on to deal with that question. The particular service a man is called to give is determined by the gifts he has received (Rom. 12:3-8). The man who would prove God's will must learn to think soberly about his own gifts. He must not think too highly of himself but understand the *measure* of the spiritual gifts of faith that have been granted him. The greater his gifts, the greater his responsibility.

This principle of stewardship in Christ's kingdom leads us to an unavoidable conclusion: *The call of the Word of God to the gospel ministry comes to ALL those who have the gifts for such a ministry.*

These gifts are bestowed by the risen Christ for the building of his church, the ingathering of the nations to his name. No man dare wrap such gifts in a napkin. In possessing this rich enduement of the Spirit a man is himself possessed. He is made debtor to all those who may hear the gospel from his lips. They cannot hear without a preacher, he cannot preach except he be sent. But if he has such gifts from Christ he *is* sent. Shall a man who is "apt to teach" be silent when the Lord commands his church to teach all nations?

There is no new principle here. A man must do all he can to serve his Saviour. The servant is not greater than his Lord: if Jesus Christ came to seek and to save that which was lost, those who are sent in his name must seek what he sought—and seeks. Not all are gifted as teachers. Many are called to work with their hands that they may provide for their families, give to the needy, and support with temporal blessings those who have labored to bring them spiritual blessings (II Thess. 3:10-12; I Thess. 4:11; Eph. 4:28; Tit. 3:8, 14 *marg.*). Such "laymen" confess Christ before men, give a reason for the faith that is in them, and by their godly lives appear as lights in the world.

But every Christian must use to the full the gifts Christ has given him for the great task of the church in the world. The man with the cheerfulness of the Spirit must visit the afflicted; the man with executive gifts must advance the order of the church; the man who is qualified of God to be a minister and teacher in the church must labor in the Word and feed the flock of Christ (Rom. 12:6-8). The fruitfulness of the greater gifts makes their unwearied use the more necessary. The preacher must be urgent in season and out of season (II Tim. 4:2). The zeal of God's house consumes him (John 2:17). His discipline as a man of God is severe. He is a soldier on service who cannot be entangled with the affairs of this life (II Tim. 2:4).

The experience of a man with the gifts for preaching is like that of the prophets of old. God's Word becomes fire in his bones (Jer. 20:9). "The lion hath roared; who will not fear? The Lord Jehovah hath spoken; who can but prophesy?" (Amos 3:8.)

Men with the gifts for the ministry have the capacity for success in other fields, but they are not free to choose them. God's first command still stands: man is to replenish the earth and subdue it; but the Great Commission takes priority over it. The Christian is a citizen of heaven, given the Word of life in a world of death. Peter left his fishing boat, Matthew left the tax business, and you must leave any calling that keeps you from exercising the gifts of the herald of Christ, if these gifts are yours. Martin Luther, like many ministers of the gospel, might have had a brilliant career in law, but the fire in his bones prevented it.

A young man was driving down a forest road in Georgia. This woodland, hundreds of thousands of acres of it, was under his supervision. His rapid rise in a large paper company had carried him from the work of a forester to a responsible position in management. He was on his way from his new dream home to a company meeting. He was thinking. With a sense of shock it came to him what he was thinking *about*. Not the production of pulpwood; not the problems of management. He was thinking about Robert, a forester and fire-control man in his employ. Was Robert a Christian? How could he reach him with the gospel? The young manager was alarmed. What was happening to him since his conversion? His fears were well-grounded. Today he is a minister of the gospel.

When he resigned his position to enter a seminary, higher management could scarcely believe that his professed reason was his real one. How could a man turn his back on such success to become a preacher? The lion had roared.

Most often the presence of such gifts of the Spirit creates a desire for their exercise. By them a man is drawn to the Word, to Christ, to men. For this reason a deep and sincere desire to enter the ministry is the commonest evidence of the Lord's calling. It is no sure criterion, however, for gifts and desire are not always joined.

A man may seek to quench the Spirit, refusing to recognize or use the gifts he has received from God (I Thess. 5:19). Samson was endued with strength for the deliverance of Israel, but he squandered his gifts and fought the Philistines only in the petty intrigues of his personal pleasure-seeking. By God's grace his tragedy ended in triumph, but Samson's desire to serve God did not match his gifts for service.

Paul had to urge Timothy not to neglect the gift that he had but to stir it up (I Tim. 4:14; II Tim. 1:6). Without exercise spiritual strength declines rapidly. Timothy must be diligent both in godly living and in vigorous teaching (I Tim. 4:12-16). He must do the work of an evangelist and fulfill his ministry (II Tim. 4:5).

Apart from the commitment of faith and a life of

obedience no man can judge of his calling to the ministry. To learn how you may serve Christ tomorrow, you must serve him today. Stir up your gifts and Christ's call will be made clear.

As gifts are used, the desire to serve Christ with them will increase. A young deacon was angry when his pastor asked him to speak at a farm where alcoholics were being rehabilitated. He refused; but when he saw tears in his minister's eyes he was ashamed and accepted. After he had spoken he learned of two men who had been deeply moved by his talk. The experience was a milestone in his call to the ministry.

On the other hand, a desire to serve Christ in the ministry may become intense before there is evidence of the necessary gifts. When Paul discusses the question of spiritual gifts with the church at Corinth, he tells them to desire earnestly the greater gifts (I Cor. 12:31). A man must think soberly in judging the gifts he has, but he may pray fervently in seeking the gifts he lacks. If his desire is pure, he may claim God's promise for greater gifts. Does he lack wisdom? Let him ask of God (James 1:5). Does he need boldness? So did the apostles, and God gave it to them in answer to prayer (Acts 4:29-31). Even Paul sought the prayers of the church that bold utterance should be given to him (Eph. 6:19). All the gifts of the Spirit are given through His presence who is giver and gift, and Christ has taught us that our heavenly Father will give the Holy Spirit to those that ask him (Luke 11:13). If you yearn to serve Christ in the gospel ministry, that desire is surely a calling to prayer for the Spirit; likely it is also a foretaste and earnest of greater gifts in store.

The buying-up of opportunities that shapes all Christian service has peculiar importance in the case of a man called to the gospel ministry. Since your calling is determined at last by your gifts, you prove your calling as you improve your gifts. No player is called to a spot on a major league team who has not proved himself in the minors. God's call *to* service normally comes *in* service. Begin with prayer. Unless your service is a living sacrifice, you cannot please God. But don't stop with prayer. Your calling will be clear as God's blessing crowns your words and deeds for him.

If we may keep the baseball metaphor, the spring training camp has its place in the discovery of pros. Seminary is for men who are seriously considering the ministry; it is a place where a man may test his gifts and calling in the service of the Word. It is often difficult for a man to be assured of his calling before the seminary experience. Has he the gifts of insight into Scripture? Can he expound the word fruitfully? The seminary classroom and study help to supply answers to such questions. The academic disciplines of theological study are no more remote from pastoral experience than the drills of the training camp from big league competition. For the man in doubt as to whether he has the teaching gift, the seminary situation may bring grateful understanding as he grows in the Word of God. Practical service, too, can be joined with learning. Summer church work, week-end opportunities, even casual encounters of personal counseling and witness can be prepared for and evaluated in the light of careful study of the Scriptures. Uncertainty about a call to the ministry may indicate with certainty a call to theological training. Even when God does not call a man to pastoral work, he often leads through seminary study to other ministries of teaching and to informed leadership in the work of the church.

Relating our gifts and our calling in consecration and wisdom is the course that Christ has laid down for his servants. Sober thought, prayerful gauging of the gifts we have received, enables us to perceive the scope and kind of ministry that is set before us. But the steward of Christ may ever seek greater gifts and pray for more power of the Spirit. In the zeal that redeems daily opportunities he brings these gifts to the proof and confesses the grace of Christ who has "wrought effectually" in him for the proclamation of the gospel.

B. YOUR CHURCH'S CALLING

Nothing can concern you more personally or intimately than your own calling of Christ. He has called you by name—not by number or by classification, for no selective service draft is so selective as Christ's. Your own new name is written on that white stone in his hand; he knows it and one day he will show it to you alone (Rev. 2:17).

Can your calling, then, be the business of anyone else? When you are assured of the Lord's call, doesn't that settle the matter? Why not present yourself to a church of your choice and inform the congregation that the Lord has called you to be their pastor?

Paul certainly insisted that he had been called directly by Christ. He was an apostle "not from men, neither through a man, but through Jesus Christ, and God the Father, who raised him from the dead" (Gal. 1:1). Must that not be your insistence, too?

Not in the same sense. The calling of an apostle as a foundation stone in the church of Christ *was* more direct than the calling of other ministers. Every apostle, Paul included, heard the voice of Jesus Christ call him by name. Christ has not appeared from heaven to you, and his call to you has come through men, in fact, through the apostles.

Yet your calling, while it may have come *through* men, has not come *from* men. In this you stand with Paul.

Christ's calling, not man's, is the source and authority of your ministry.

How then can the calling of men be related to the calling of Christ? Paul's discussion in the Epistle to the Galatians gives us further help. His calling of Christ was surely direct and immediate. But even Paul was formally recognized by the "pillars" of the church. James, Peter, and John gave him the right hand of fellowship that he might go to the Gentiles with the gospel (Gal. 2:9). Paul rightly insists that this recognition added nothing to the authority he had been given by Christ. Yet it was a proper recognition, in harmony with the order of the church.

The key to this action is described by Paul in these words: "when they perceived the grace that was given unto me" (Gal. 2:9). This is the principle that relates the calling of men to the calling of Christ. Christ gives the grace, and with the grace the calling. But men of spiritual discernment may perceive the presence of such grace in the life of a disciple. When the church sees the evidence of Christ's calling it not only may, but should recognize this publicly.

The same gifts of the Spirit that give assurance to the man of God regarding his own calling also mark him out to the people of God. The church does not call in its own name, but in Christ's. The function of the church is to recognize and acknowledge the calling of God. "He that wrought for Peter unto the apostleship of the circumcision wrought for me also unto the Gentiles," writes Paul (Gal. 2:8). The ascended Lord calls men by the gifts of his Spirit. The man called is steward of these gifts; he dare not quench the Spirit. The stewardship is not his only, however. His gifts are for use in the body of Christ, ministering to the upbuilding of the whole body in the full maturity of Christ (Eph. 4:11-16).

The church must claim these gifts and provide channels for their use; it must also respect and honor them as gifts of Christ. We have seen that gifts of authority require public recognition for their proper exercise. A man may love or pray secretly but he can govern or admonish only openly. The recognition of the church does not bestow the authority: only the gift of Christ can do that. It does accept the authority and relate the gifts of one man of God to the gifts of the people of God so that the mutual sharing and fellowship of gifts may minister to the growth of Christ's body.

In the book of Acts evidences of this role of the church abound. The community at Jerusalem determines which two candidates have the qualifications for being numbered with the twelve in the place of Judas (Acts 1:23). When the requirements for the ministry of the seven are given by the apostles, the church chooses men who have these spiritual gifts (Acts 6:3). Paul and the other missionaries of the Church at Antioch, though called of the Spirit, are separated to their work and sent by the prophets and teachers of the church (Acts 13:1-3). In the same way Timothy was ordained for his work by the presbytery (I Tim 4:14; II Tim. 1:6).

Of course the "setting apart" of the church is done in prayer, and in the blessing of the Saviour's name. Further grace is given of God to seal this dedication to service (I Tim. 4:14). But the church does not choose out a man and then proceed to equip him with spiritual endue-ment. It seeks for the man or men God has chosen whether through direct prophecy (Acts 9:15, 16; 13:2; I Tim. 1:18; 4:14) or through the perception of his gifts (Gal. 2:9).

The public recognition of the gifts of Christ is not the whole of the church's responsibility. The orderly exercise of the gifts must also be sought. Because Christ plants his gifts in a body they can only function properly in fellowship, and fellowship requires order. Christians with the gift of tongues at Corinth forgot the principle of edifying fellowship and turned the blessings of Pentecost into something like the curse of Babel. A man with a real gift of Christ cannot demand an immediate exercise of his gift under all circumstances. He must wait his turn, or even be silent (I Cor. 14:26-33).

That applies even to preachers. Just as the seven "deacons" of Acts had their gifts before they were called by the church to a place of public duty, so any man of God may be equipped for ministry before he is given full scope for service. Young men find it hard to wait for God's season, but God always joins the man and the moment in perfect wisdom.

The ordering of Christian fellowship often includes the *where* as well as the *when* of Christian service. The church recognized that the gifts granted to Peter and Paul distinguished the area of their ministry. Both had full apostolic authority, but one was sent particularly to the Jews and the other to the Gentiles (Gal. 2:7-10). The expressed needs of the churches that sought the apostle's ministry played a significant part in determining the places where Paul and his fellow-workers labored (Phil. 2:12, 19-25; II Cor. 1:15-23).

Neither the minister or the church may arbitrarily ignore the insights of the other as to the gifts and calling of God. The church that seeks in advance the pledge of a missionary candidate to go wherever the board may send him and to do whatever the board may assign is guilty of at least a bureaucratic oversimplification of Christ's calling. On the other hand, the candidate who seeks with agonizing earnestness to discover in secret prayer the exact place to which the Lord would have him go may be isolating himself from the appointed means of discovering that place. He cannot ignore the counsel of his Christian brothers: where does the church find the greatest need for a man of his evident gifts?

Christ's calling draws us to our brethren as well as to our Saviour. We are to exercise our calling in the fellowship of the church; we must find it there too. Take the towel and basin and discover your calling at your brother's feet; go with him to visit the prisoner and find your calling at his side. You may be convinced of your calling to the ministry long before others mark your gifts, but if you are diligent in the fellowship of the gospel your profiting will appear to all; Christ's calling will be acknowledged by Christ's church. Or it may be that your first inkling of the call of Christ came from the lips of a fellow Christian who saw the evidences of the Lord's blessing on your life. Whether your calling was first apparent to you or to your brethren is not of decisive importance. Christ's gospel is preached today by hundreds who yearned for the ministry from childhood and hundreds more who fought their calling with a rising panic while their friends prayed. What is important is that your own awareness of Christ's gifts should be joined with the perception of the church.

To this end there is no substitute for regular fellowship. On the day that you are set apart to minister Christ's Word you will be in the midst of his people. The parts of that service require the communion of the saints: a worshiping congregation, men of God preaching, praying, extending hands of blessing and of fellowship in the gospel. That service would be a curious way to seal a solitary calling. You are not first set by Christ in the midst of his church on the day of your ordination. You need your fellow-Christians now, and they need you. Private soul-searching is not enough to determine your call to the ministry. The judgment of the people of God must be sought; long before the time when it must be given formally it should be sought informally. Welcome the counsel and criticism of your pastor and your Christian friends. Above all, remember Paul's favorite figure of the athlete. Your gifts will become evident on the field. Neither private meditation nor personal counseling can prove your calling. That comes with God's blessing on your active service in the body of Christ.

Of course the necessary ministry of church fellowship must be found in Christ. There is no fellowship of righteousness with iniquity, no communion of light with darkness, no concord of Christ with Belial. Young men sometimes distrust ecclesiastical counsel with good reason. When the power of church order is turned to the service of another gospel a spiritual tyranny arises that offers stumblingblocks rather than stepping-stones to the candidate for the ministry. Never were the warnings of the Pastoral Epistles against false teachers more needed than today. Yet a man must no more allow the existence of false churches to drive him from the true than he would allow the existence of false Christs to drive him from the Saviour.

To prove your calling your fellowship must be with the Son of God and with the sons of God.

Are you called to the ministry? If you have been called out of darkness into Christ's light you are surely called to *ministry*. You must do all in your power to show forth his praises who called you to follow him. If you refuse to minister to the sick and imprisoned you are refusing Christ. If you care nothing for men lost in sin you do not know the love of Christ or the joy of heaven when the lost are found.

The question then is only this: what has God put in your power to do in his service? What you *can* do you *must* do, and find yourself at best an unprofitable servant.

89

Have you the gifts for the gospel ministry? Then Christ has set before you an open door that no man can shut. To you it is given to bear fruit not thirty, nor sixty, but a hundredfold.

The harvest is plentiful, the laborers are few. Pray the Lord of the harvest and go forth in his name. He that has begun a good work in you will perfect it until the day of Jesus Christ (Phil. 1:6). Jesus prayed all night before he called the twelve (Luke 6:12, 13). He intercedes in heaven as he calls you, praying that though you be sifted as wheat your faith will not fail, but that you may become his chosen vessel to bear his name before the nations.